WORLD FOOD SUMMIT

Editor
DR. DIGUMARTI BHASKARA RAO
M.Sc., M.A., M.A., M.Ed., Ph.D.

Secretary
**Academy of Communication, Culture
Education, Science and Service**
*D-43, Srinivasa Nagar Colony
Guntur - 522 006
Andhra Pradesh
India*

1997
**DISCOVERY PUBLISHING HOUSE
NEW DELHI**

Reprinted - 2014

ISBN: 978-81-7141-386-7

World Food Summit

Published by:
DISCOVERY PUBLISHING HOUSE PVT. LTD.
4383/4B, Ansari Road, Darya Ganj
New Delhi-110 002 (India)
Phone: +91-11-23279245, 43596064-65
Fax: +91-11-23253475
E-mail: discoverypublishinghouse@gmail.com
sales@discoverypublishinggroup.com
web: www.discoverypublishinggroup.com

Printed at:
Infinity Imaging Systems
Delhi

CONTENTS

Preface VII

Acknowledgements IX

1. Introduction 1
2. Seeds of Life 9
3. Plan, Protect and Produce 14
4. After the Harvest is in 20
5. Towards a New Green Revolution 26
6. Aquaculture Offers Cause for Hope 32
7. Forests and Nutrition 37
8. Women Feed the World 42
9. Water and Food Security 47
10. Livestock and Food Security 53
11. Agriculture and Food Security 59
12. Agricultural Research and Food Security 66
13. Fisheries and Food Security 72
14. Forests and Food Security 77
15. Environment and Food Security 83

16. Rome Declaration on World Food Security 89

17. World Food Summit Plan of Action 94

PREFACE

The World Food Summit held during November 13-17, 1996 at the Rome headquarters of the Food and Agricultural Organisation of the United Nations brought on to a common platform the heads of State and Government or their representatives to renew high-level commitment around the world to the eradication of hunger and malnutrition and to the achievement of lasting food security for all people, and also to turn their attention to the question of food security - how to ensure that all their citizens have access to the food they need to live healthy and productive lives.

The Heads of State and Government have adopted the Rome Declaration on World Food Security and World Food Summit Plan of Action. In Rome Declaration, the Heads of State and Government or their representatives reaffirmed the right of everyone to have access to safe and nutritious food, consistent with the right to adequate food and the fundamental right of everyone to be free from hunger; pledged their political will and their common and national commitment to achieving the food security for all; reaffirmed that a peaceful stable and enabling political, social and economic environment is the essential foundation which will enable States to give adequate priority to food security and poverty eradication; determined to make efforts to mobilize, and optimize the allocation and utilization of technical and financial resources from all sources, to reinforce national actions to implement sustainable food security policies; and pledged their actions and support to implement the World Food Summit Plan of Action. The Rome Declaration and the Summit's Plan of Action laid the foundations for diverse paths to a common objective - food security, at the individual, household, national, regional and global levels. In the Plan of Action, the seven commitments made were explained with their specific objectives and actions. The Declaration and Plan of Action aim at food security.

This book on the World Food Summit presents before the readers the documents related to the food security developed by various divisions of Food and Agriculture Organisation of the United Nations either independently or in association with the other United Nations agencies and bodies and the full texts of the Rome Declaration on World Food Security and World Food Summit Plan of Action which were approved by the Committee on World Food Security and submitted to the World Food Summit for adoption. These documents may help many researchers, policy-makers, political leaders and even social service activists in bringing food security and in removing the problems such as malnutrition, hunger and poverty.

We hope for the bright future of the mankind.

Dr. D. Bhaskara Rao
Republic Day, 1997

ACKNOWLEDGEMENTS

I

Express my Cordial thanks

and

a deep sense of appreciation

to

Food and Agricultural Organisation

United Nations

Secretariat of the World Food Summit

Director-General of FAO

FAO Representative in India

United Nations Environment Programme

NGOs' Forums and Organisations

and

Heads of State or Government

who

made this publication possible

for the benefit of

agriculturists, policy-makers, leaders and activists

Dr. D. B. RAO
ACCESS

1

WORLD FOOD SUMMIT INTRODUCTION

The **World Food Summit** - from 13 to 17 November 1996—brought together Heads of State and Government and other world leaders at the Rome Headquarters of the Food and Agriculture Organization of the United Nations (FAO). The objective of the Summit was to renew high-level commitment around the world to the eradication of hunger and malnutrition and to the achievement of lasting food security for all people.

The Summit represented the *first time in history* that the world's Heads of State and Government gathered to turn their attention to the question of "food security" - how to ensure that all their citizens have access to the food they need to live healthy, productive lives.

Why a Summit ?

As the year 2000 approaches, human society can be justly proud of its record of scientific and technological achievement. But in spite of these advances, hundreds of millions of people live in chronic hunger of malnutrition. World cereal stocks are at their lowest levels since the early 1970s, with sharp price rises as a result. Food aid has declined by almost half in the last three years.

Looking to the future, today's global population of more than 5.7 billion is projected to increase by another 3 billion by the year 2030, placing still greater pressure on finite natural resources. The per person availability of land suitable for agriculture and fresh water is declining as the world's population expands.

There is increasing awareness of the relationship between lack of access to food and water on the one hand, and political instability and uncontrolled migration of people on the other.

Access to Food - Where We Stand Today ?

In the developing countries alone, more than 800 million people today face chronic undernutrition, and 200 million children under the age of five suffer from chronic calorie and protein deficiencies. Unless determined action is taken, the number of chronically undernourished people might still be about 700 million in the year 2010, with over 260 million of them in sub-Saharan Africa.

At present, as many as 82 nations fall into category of low-income food-deficit countries (LIFDCs): 41 in Sub-Saharan Africa, 19 in Asia and the Pacific, 9 in Europe/ Commonwealth of independent States, 7 in Latin America and Caribbean, and 6 in Near East/North Africa. Rising prices in the international grains market have serious consequences for these countries which have to import cereals to meet their domestic food needs.

Growing Concern

At the 1974 World Food Conference, Governments examined the global problem of food production and consumption, and solemnly proclaimed that "every man, woman and child has the inalienable right to be free from hunger and malnutrition in order to develop their physical and mental faculties".

More than 20 years later, though, the Conference's goal of eradicating hunger, food insecurity and malnutrition "within a decade", has not been reached.

Since the World Food Conference, a number of major conferences have addressed certain problems related to food security in the context of their particular agendas; but world leaders at the highest level have not had the opportunity to assess the state of global food security and focus their collective attention specifically on securing this most basic of human needs.

At the 27th Session of the FAO Conference in November 1993, which met at the Ministerial level, Member Nations expressed "deep concern" at the present situation and the future prospects, and stressed that "the world's major problems in food, nutrition and sustainability require immediate action at national and international levels".

The Summit Initiative

Against this background, the Director General of FAO consulted a large number of Heads of State and Government from all regions of the World. He found an emerging consensus on the need to convene a World Food Summit as early as possible, in order to renew the commitment to achieving food security for all and agree upon effective policies and strategies for dealing with the root causes of hunger and malnutrition - now, and in the decades to come. At its 28th Session in October 1995 the FAO Conference - comprising 174 Members - called for the convening of a World Food Summit at the level of Heads of State or Government, in Rome in November 1996. During the preceding months, growing support for the Summit had been confirmed by discussions at the 106th, 107th and 108th Sessions of the FAO Council and FAO Regional Conferences, as well as by resolutions and recommendations adopted at numerous other intergovernmental meetings. In December 1995, the Summit received the unanimous endorsement of the United Nations General Assembly.

The Government of Italy pledged its material and diplomatic support to the organization for the convening of a successful Summit, and Confirmed its readiness to cooperate fully in every appropriate area, and acted accordingly.

The Summit Expectations

Heads of State and Government attending the Summit were expected to adopt a Declaration and 'lan of Action for achieving food security.

As envisaged, this was a seven-point plan stipulating concrete practical actions to ensure: 1. Conditions conducive to food security, 2. Access to food by all, 3. Sustainable increases in food production, 4. Trade's contribution to food security, 5. Emergency relief when and where needed, 6. The required investments, and 7. Concerted efforts to achieve results by countries and organizations, individually and collectively.

A meeting of the World's Heads of State and Government, for any reason, was an extraordinary occasion. The high visibility of the summit has raised awareness among decision-makers in the public and private sectors, in the media and with the public at large. More importantly, Heads of State and Government have the influence, capacity and authority to spur change in many sectors. Their personal participation in the Summit is a recognition of the multiple dimensions of food security.

Not only Ministers of Agriculture (who meet regularly every two years at the FAO Conference) and related technical departments (fisheries, forestry, environment, water resources, rural development), but also Ministries of Foreign Affairs, Trade, Economy, Development Cooperation, and others have played important roles in ensuring food security.

State, provincial and local authorities were also involved, along with the organizations of civil society and the private sector.

No New Bureaucracy

The World Food Summit was not intended to be a

pledging conference, nor was it aimed at creating new financial mechanisms, institutions or bureaucracy. After the Summit, each participating nation will consider independently how it can achieve the objectives set out in the plan of action adopted by the Summit. International organizations, NGOs and others were also invited to be part of an international effort to eliminate chronic hunger.

High Impact, But Low Cost

The Summit has been carefully planned in order to keep costs to a minimum, while at the same time ensuring sound preparation in terms of physical arrangements and logistics, technical and policy documents, and consultation with governments, NGOs, the private sector, the academic and research communities, and other intergovernmental organizations including the UN system organizations and the Bretton Woods institutions.

- The regularly scheduled sessions of FAO's Governing Bodies have been utilized for Summit preparations to hold down the expenses connected with preparatory meetings.
- The Summit was held in Rome, at FAO's Headquarters, using existing conference facilities and services, avoiding the costs associated with holding such a meeting away from Headquarters.
- The organizational work has been entrusted to a small Secretariat of staff seconded from other FAO departments, who returned to their normal work after the Summit.
- While the minimum, basic costs of holding the Summit were being financed by FAO's Regular Programme, voluntary contributions in cash and kind were used to cover other costs, in particular to encourage wide participation from developing countries and for related NGO activities. Donations have come from governments, organizations, foundations and the private sector.
- Participations were encouraged to avoid holding receptions and dinners and to donate any funds which would

have been used for such hospitality to the financing of the Special Programme for Food Production in Support of Low Income Food-Deficit Countries.

The Preparatory Process

The preparatory process has been designed to include broad-based consultations with governments, inter-governmental and non-governmental organizations, and the private sector. FAO's Committee on World Food Security (CFS) overseen the Summit preparatory process.

Through a special inter-sessional working group, it has focused in particular on the development and negotiation of the draft Summit documents. The aim was to complete the negotiation of these documents and send an agreed text to national capitals in October 1996.

Numerous inter-governmental organizations have lent their formal support to the World Food Summit, and called for top-level participation on the part of governments. Resolutions were passed, for example, by the Organization of African Unity, the Organization of the Islamic Conference, the Inter-Parliamentary Union, CARICOM and many others.

Dozens of other fora have contributed to the Summit process, beginning with a Global Assembly on Food Security, and an International Symposium organized by the Federal Government of Canada and the Government of Quebec in October 1995 in Quebec. These sessions preceded the Ministerial Meeting on World Food Security convened in Quebec on the occasion of the 50th Anniversary of FAO - founded in Quebec City, Canada in 1945.

Countries and organizations have been encouraged to use other meetings already scheduled within their regions to discuss the specific implications of food security issues.

NGOs have been encouraged to participate in national-level activities and in NGO consultations organized prior to each FAO Regional Conference and 22nd Session of the Committee on the World Food Security.

NGOs around the World have also been organized their own meetings to discuss the Summit. Several important NGO Declarations for the World Food Summit have been submitted to the Summit Secretariat.

Technical Underpinning for Political Decisions

The World Food Summit Series of technical background papers comprises the following titles :

Synthesis of the technical background documents

Food, agriculture and food security: developments since the World Food Conference and prospects for the future

Success stories in food security

Socio-political and economic environment for food security

Food requirements and population growth

Food security and nutrition

Lessons from the Green Revolution: towards a new green revolution

Food production : the critical role of water

Food for consumers : marketing, processing and distribution

Role of research in global food security and agricultural development

Investment in agriculture: evolution and prospects

Food production and environmental impact

Food and international trade

Food security and food assistance

Assessment of feasible progress in food security

Technical atlas

At the Summit ....

The World Food Summit took place at FAO Headquarters in Rome from 13 to 17 November 1996. The Summit's format allowed for sequential statements by observers and government delegations, culminating in its second half with the interventions by Heads of State or Government.

A series of Summit Circulars was used to keep government delegations informed of the details arrangements for their participation. NGOs were kept informed through a series of NGO information notes.

Parallel Events

In addition to the NGO Forum, a number of other groups organized meetings and events in parallel with or around the time of the World Food Summit. These included farmers' organizations, youth groups, parliamentarians, scientists and academics, private sector associations and others.

Achievement

The Heads of State and Government have adopted the Rome Declaration on World Food Security and World Food Summit Plan Of Action.

2

SEEDS OF LIFE

The crops used for food and agriculture at present are the product of years of natural evolution, selection by farmers and scientific plant breeding. But, today, the diversity of plant species is subject to serious threats, among them pollution, resource degradation, destruction of habitats and alteration of ecosystems. Loss of species irreversibly reduces the genetic store on which future crop improvement and adaptability depends.

Plants' Contribution to Food Security

Before the rise of the earliest civilizations, our ancestors were identifying, developing and using plant genetic resources, favouring certain wild plants over others for their unique characteristics and selecting those most suited to their needs. Slowly, these practices have led to the domestication of virtually all of the agricultural species we depend on today for food, feed, flavoring, fibre, materials for shelter, fertilizers, fuel and medicines. Even so, cultivated crops represent a very small portion of what is available in nature.

Of the several hundred thousand known plant species, some 120 are cultivated for human food. But just nine of these crops supply over 75 percent of global plant-derived energy intake and of those, only three - wheat, rice and maize - account for more than 50 per

cent. At the local level, however, many less commercial crops are important for subsistence. An estimated 80 percent of the vitamin A and more than a third of the vitamin C in the diet of Africa's people are supplied by traditional food plants.

Forest dwellers, who use at least 1300 plant species for medical and related purposes, have contributed to the discovery of an estimated three-quarters of the plant-derived prescription drugs widely used in the developed world today. The active ingredients found in 25 percent of prescription drugs come from plants.

The Importance of Biological Diversity

The Genes found in large untapped wealth of undomesticated plants can provide the key to the improved crops we will need to feed the world's population in the future. **For example, during the 1970s, the grassy-stunt virus devastated rice fields from India to Indonesia, endangering the world's single most important food crop. A gene from an Indian wild relative was used to confer resistance to varieties that are new grown across 11 million ha of Asian rice fields.**

Genetic diversity helps crops to withstand changes in environment, climate and agricultural methods as well as threats from pests and diseases. In each of the Planet's diverse ecosystems, biological diversity is at root of a complex ecological balance.

Genetic Erosion

The Chief Cause of loss of genetic diversity - referred to as genetic erosion - has been the spread of modern, commercial agriculture. **The introduction of new, highly uniform varieties has resulted in the loss of traditional farmers' varieties**. Unfortunately, genetic erosion is almost always associated with - or even preceded by - loss of the knowledge regarding varieties and their uses.

Genetic erosion reduces the material available for use in plant improvement. At the same time, uniformity

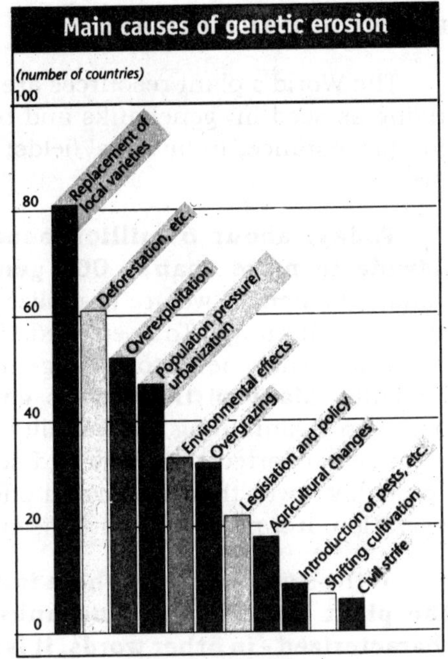

makes crops much more vulnerable to changes in the presence of pests and diseases by narrowing their genetic base - the stockpile of characteristics that can provide crucial resistance or immunity.

Deforestation is a major cause of loss of species, be they plant or animal. It has been estimated that the clearing of closed tropical rainforests could account for the loss of as many as 100 species each day. **Deforestation will be the single greatest cause of special loss in the next 50 years.**

Loss of Plant Genetic Resources

- In China, of the nearly 10 000 wheat varieties in use in 1949, only 1 000 remained by the 1970s.
- In the Unites States, 95 percent of the cabbage, 91 percent of the field maize, 94 per cent of the pea, 86 per cent of the apple and 81 per cent of the tomato varieties cultivated in the last century have been lost.
- The Andean countries are experiencing large-scale erosion of local varieties of indigenous crops and crop wild relatives that were important sources of protein and vitamins for their ancestors.
- At present, uniformity in the rootstock of California wine grapes and the resulting susceptibility to a virulent disease is causing wine producers to dig up and replace their vines at the cost of hundreds of millions of dollars.

Conserving our Heritage

The World's plant resources are found either *ex situ,* including as seed in genebanks and botanical gardens, or *in situ,* for instance, in farmers' fields, on rangelands or in forests.

Today, about 6 million accessions are stored worldwide in more than 1 000 genebanks. But much remains to be done if we are to realize the full value of our plant genetic heritage. To keep seeds in genebanks viable, for instance, they need to be regenerated and regrown periodically. Many of the world's genebanks are facing problems in maintaining seed quality. In a recent survey, 77 countries reported that they had seed storage facilities, but probably fewer than half could offer secure, long term conservation and management of seeds.

At the same time, **anywhere from 80 to 95 per cent of the plant material in genebanks worldwide is still uncharacterized - in other words, it is still unknown what these seeds may contain in their genetic makeup.** This information is fundamental if we are to use this material to produce better crops, both through traditional breeding methods and by applying advance biotechnological techniques.

Farmers continue to play a key role in maintaining biological diversity. **Globally, 1.5 billion farmers are involved**

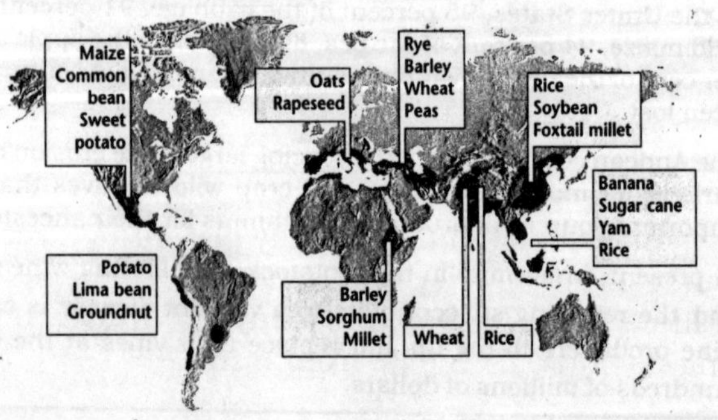

Centres of Origin of Some Common Crops

in on-farm conservation and breeding, selecting varieties and improving crops on a day-to-day basis. But most of the farm families that are responsible for this type of management and improvement of plant genetic resources are limited by lack of resources.

Making the Most of What We Have

Efforts to make the most of the world's plant genetic resources must concentrate on three basic spheres of activity:

- Conservation, documentation and sharing the genetic resources available;
- Use of these resources in a way that is sustainable and that will not further jeopardize the ecology;
- Fair and equitable distribution of benefits, including among countries, private interests and farmers.

Well-founded efforts to tap the wide array of plant

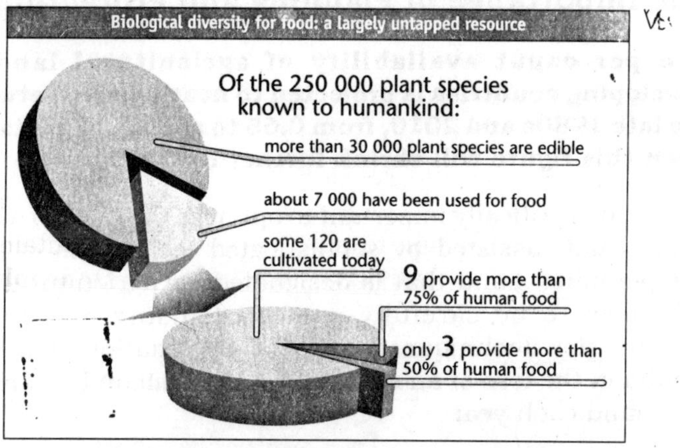

genetic resources, including carefully planned conservation, management and distribution schemes, can allow these seeds of life to play a major role today and in the future, in protecting millions of people from hunger.

3

PLAN, PROTECT AND PRODUCE

As the available agricultural land per head of population dwindles, countries must plan how best to use their land. Sound methods of preventing land degradation must then be applied so that production can be maximized without jeopardizing future fertility.

The Importance of Planning and Protection

The per caput availability of agricultural land in developing countries is projected to nearly halve between the late 1980s and 2010, from 0.65 to about 0.4 hectares. Even this figure will shrink further by 2050.

It is critically important to optimize the uses to which land is put, assisted by sophisticated techniques of land use planning. Land that is designated for agricultural use will have to be carefully protected, using a range of conservation techniques, from the degradation that now results in the loss of an estimated 5 to 7 million hectares of good land each year.

Most land users do not have the time, the resources or the inclination to adopt new, and perhaps risky, practices to tackle problems that they probably cannot even see. So emphasis must be placed on involving farmers from the start in developing and adopting measures that not only conserve the soil but also offer short-term, tangible benefits —such as increased yields or easier work.

Matching the Land to the Use

Sound land-use planning has been made much easier by the advent of micro-computers, the development of databases and the use of Geographic Information systems (GIS), see diagram on page 16.

The diagram below summarizes the essential steps in optimizing the choice of crop for any given plot of land, down to a 10-km square. These steps involve matching the requirements of individual crops (step 1) with existing conditions on the ground : climatic requirements (2a) and soil requirements (2b). Overlaying these two inventories then creates a land inventory which includes information on both climate and soil (3). Constraints on crop yield are then added on, together with information about pests and harvesting difficulties (4). Finally, data on soil constraints are added, resulting in a land-use recommendation about what crop should be grown, what inputs will be required. and what crop managements techniques should be used.

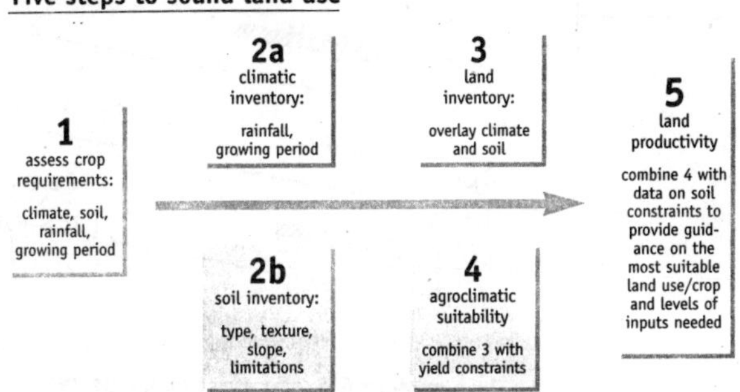

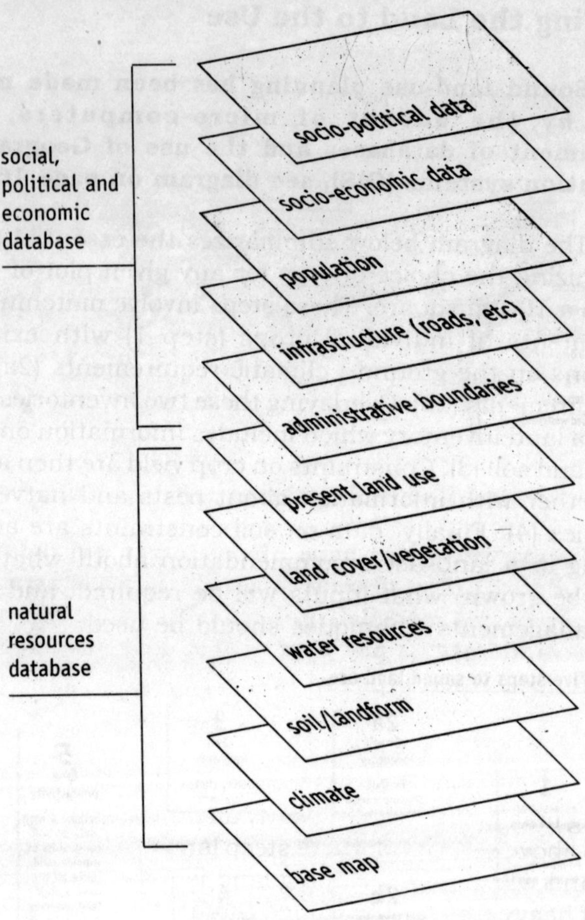

In a modern GIS, the exact geographical location of each piece of data stored in a database is recorded. For each geographical location, the required data can then be called up, and layers of information built up one over the other. The resulting map can then either be viewed on screen or printed out.

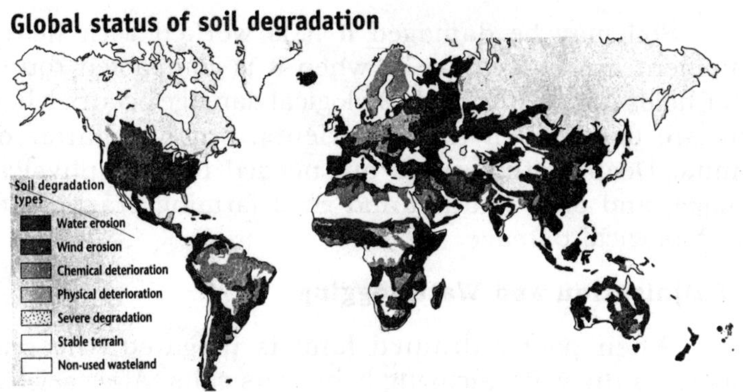

The Causes of Land Degradation

Human activities have often led to degradation of the world's land resources. Damage has occurred on 15 percent of the world's total land area - 13 per cent light and moderate, 2 per cent severe and very severe. There are four main types of land degradation.

- **Water Erosion**

The commonest form of degradation, water erosion is causing massive damage in nearly all developing countries (see map above). It occurs where steep land is being unwisely farmed and where gently sloping land is left exposed to the effects of heavy rain. In the United States the annual loss of topsoil still averages 12 tonnes per hectare, and an estimated 50 million tonnes a year of plant nutrients are washed away with it.

- **Wind Erosion**

Land stripped of vegetation and exposed to strong winds can be quickly blown away - as much as 150 tonnes can be blown off one hectare in an hour. Wind erosion caused the famous dust bowls in the Great Plains of the United States in the 1930s. The cure for wind erosion is to ensure good ground cover and windbreaks (such as hedges).

■ Physical and Biological Damage

Soil may be damaged if it is worked with heavy equipment in wet weather or when it is compacted round water holes in pasture land. Biological damage occurs when soils are deprived of their nutrients, organic matter or humus. Deep-rooting crops are needed to cure physical damage, and crop rotation and good farming practices to cure biological damage.

■ Salinization and Waterlogging

When poorly drained land is irrigated, the sun evaporates the water, leaving behind its salts. After several years, the soil becomes highly saline and affects plant growth. If drainage is very poor, the soil may also become waterlogged. It is estimated that about 40 million out of 200 million irrigated hectares are waterlogged, affected by salt, or both. The area of land being abandoned every year for these reasons is roughly equal to the amount of land being reclaimed and irrigated.

Land Degradation : Key Facts

- The major causes of soil degradation are mismanagement of arable land (28 percent), overgazing (36 percent) and deforestation (35 percent).
- Efficient soil conservation would enable many countries to support populations 50 percent greater than with unchecked soil erosion.
- In Costa Rica application of 53 land use recommendations boosted maize production from 2.76 to 3.68 tonnes/hectare without increased fertilization.
- Proper crop management is the best form of erosion control, capable of reducing soil losses from 100 to 5 tonnes/hectare/year.
- After the dust bowls of the 1930s, US officials planted 220 million trees as 'nets to catch the wind'.
- In Niger's Keita Valley, a major FAO soil conservation project has transformed a barren landscape into a flourishing environment which can be seen from space as a green patch in the desert.

Stopping the Damage

Checking land degradation depends on two simple ideas: first, the prevention of degradation carries with it its own motivating force - the increase in production that accompanies well protected land; and, second, that land users can and will organize and implement the necessary measures themselves, given a little catalytic help. These are bold new ideas, contrasting starkly with traditional conservation techniques which were imposed from above and required expensive and exhausting physical labour. Today the emphasis is on biological techniques - such as preserving ground cover and choosing the right crop for the right land - and crop management methods that avoid degradation from the start.

4

AFTER THE HARVEST IS IN

Efficient marketing, processing and distribution systems can make a vital contribution to food security by helping to ensure that people have access to the food they need, at prices they can afford. At the same time, post-harvest activities make an important contribution to national employment and income.

The Food Chain

The food chain that stretches from the farm to the table is made up of many links. If any one of these is broken or obstructed, the effect on prices and availability of food can be drastic. Often, the severest consequences are felt by the poorest families.

A large share of the food produced in developing countries never reaches the consumers. In many countries, a virtual absence of support services and marketing information impedes effective decision-making about planting, harvesting or processing. Farmers may produce crops in excess of the actual demand, or they may all produce at one time, flooding the market. The lack of appropriate storage and processing facilities and techniques prevents preservation of seasonal surpluses.

Farmers' investments in production become more costly and risky when marketing, storage and distribution are inefficient. When local markets are lacking, for instance, produce cannot be sold. The rural markets that do exist often lack basic infrastructure such as shelter from the spoilage and in contamination, with consequent health risks.

Transport often represents a major component of the final cost of the food. Prices can become prohibitive when transport costs exceed the value of the producer. Spoilage rates soar when trucks taking produce to market must slowly navigate around potholes on crumbling rural roads. Bad roads also cause greater wear and tear on vehicles, the cost of which is ultimately borne by consumers.

Where the consumers will be

Urban and rural population projections in developing countries
Millions (percentage of population)

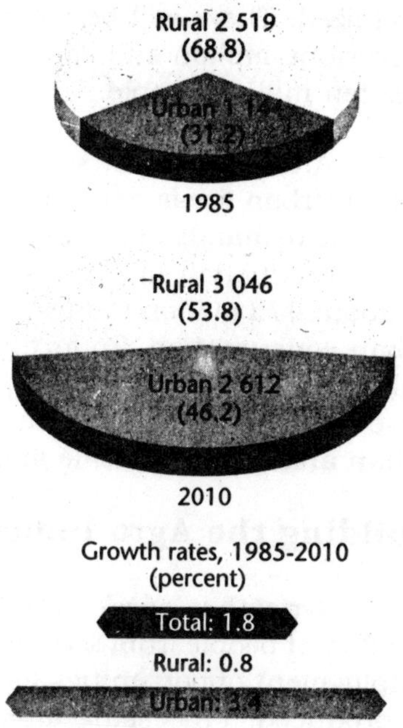

Rural 2 519
(68.8)
Urban 1 14
(31.2)
1985

Rural 3 046
(53.8)
Urban 2 612
(46.2)
2010

Growth rates, 1985-2010
(percent)
Total: 1.8
Rural: 0.8
Urban: 3.4

Explosive urban growth presents challenges for food supply and distribution, as a shrinking rural population must feed an expanding city population.

Markets Make a Difference

Aside from making food readily available, rural markets enhance local food security by providing a source of income for agricultural and non-agricultural labourers and artisans. In the cities, markets provide access to a diversified food supply throughout the year. The importance of marketing, processing and distribution is expected to increase with growing urban populations. Between 1985 and 2010, it is estimated that rural populations in developing countries will grow annually by 0.8 per cent, while those of the cities will expand by 3.4 per cent. This will mean that the year 2010, all the major world regions will be heavily urbanized. There will be some 200 cities with populations of over one million and 21 "megacities" with populations of over ten million people.

Although much scope remains for food production in peri-urban areas and home gardens, most of the food to meet the demands of the cities will come from more distant areas. Production of cereals alone is expected to increase by about 472 million tonnes, a good part of which will be for urban consumption. To fortify the food chain, rural-urban linkages will have to be improved and new markets will have to emerge - in producing areas, for assembly, and in urban areas for wholesale and retail sales.

Building the Agro-Industry

Growth in agro-related industries can help to reduce the flow of people from the countries to the cities by creating employment opportunities for them close to where the food is produced. Processing already provides employment for millions of rural people, in particular women, for whom it is often the main source of income. Innovative, cost-effective and simple processing techniques can also make an enormous difference in food availability, reducing post-harvest losses, providing an outlet for surplus food, and allowing the poor to make it through periods of food security. In addition, processing allows for greater variety in the diet and can help alleviate problems of disease by improving food safety.

What Women - and Their Families - Have to Gain

In most developing countries, women are heavily involved in all phases of post harvest activity. Improvement in marketing, processing and distribution systems will not only better their lot. It will most certainly be reflected in improvements in the food security of their households.

Studies show that women spend a significant part of their income - proportionately much higher than the amount spent by men - on food for the family.

As more and more men migrate to the cities in search of employment, the availability of good-quality, affordable processed food can help to ease women's heavy workload, lessening the time and energy needed for the meal preparation.

Information : As Important as Seed and Plow

Marketing, processing and distribution are dynamic processes that must be responsive to the changing environment in which food is produced and consumed. Evolving cultural patterns, fashions, domestic priorities and many other factors can affect demand for food, while a host of natural and man-made circumstances determine its availability.

Adequate information flows help to ensure that improved post-harvest systems are geared to real needs and demands, and are both economically and socially feasible. Feedback on consumers' need and preferences helps farmers to make better informed decisions about planting, harvest and, in the case of some forest products, gathering and selling.

Reliable market information allows them to tailor supply to match demand, minimizing food wastage and financial losses that result from over-production.

On the other hand, technical innovations must be carefully studied to avoid negative impact, especially on women and on the poor. In one African country, for example, the arrival of village-based threshing and winnowing machines meant the loss of traditional "gleaning" rights for the women who had previously carried out this work manually. Information on users and their needs can help to ensure that technologies are appropriate within the circumstances of the areas where they are introduced.

A Marketing Case Study: Potatoes in Bangladesh

The history of potato production in Bangladesh underlines the importance of post-harvest systems. In 1990, the Government of Bangladesh - with assistance from Canada and the Netherlands—set up a programme to expand production of potatoes and other vegetables. By 1993/94, potato yields had risen from 10.0 to 18.1 million tonnes per hectare, much of which was consumed by the farm families that grew them.

Major problems ensued, however, as potato production continued to expand. Insufficient attention had been paid to the post-harvest system from the outset. Demand for potatoes among non-farm families was not high enough to absorb production during the particularly prolific 1994/1995 season, and storage facilities for the surplus were seriously wanting. As a result, many farmers experienced losses and even stopped growing the crop.

The Role of Government

While it is generally recognised that direct intervention in produce marketing is not the best way to support farmers, indirect support is necessary, especially in countries undergoing structural changes that affect the post-harvest systems. Farmers continue to rely heavily on governments to:

- improve rural marketing infrastructure;
- improve and maintain roads;
- provide marketing information services;
- ensure access to information on food processing and preservation techniques;
- strengthen extension services;
- set and monitor quality and safety standards for food;
- develop associations representing farmers, consumers, traders and processors;
- promote economically viable investment.

Most important is to ensure a clear stable policy and macro-economic environment in which the private sector can rapidly respond to opportunities.

For the poor and the hungry, improvements in the efficiency of the food chain are vital measures that can make the difference in their day-today subsistence, enabling them to break the vicious circle of hunger and poverty.

5

TOWARDS A NEW GREEN REVOLUTION

By the year 2010, the population of the planet is expected to swell to around 7 billion, almost double what it had been just 40 years earlier. If present trends continue, nearly one person in 10, or some 680 million people, will still suffer from chronic undernutrition. Reversing these trends without clearing and plowing vast areas of marginal lands and irreplaceable natural habitats will require rapid and sustainable gains in agricultural production - a new green revolution.

Why a New Green Revolution

In the regions inhabited by the majority of humanity, most land suitable for agriculture is already being farmed. Significant areas that could be opened up for agriculture do exist in Africa and Latin America. But most are covered by forest. Converting them for agriculture would take a heavy toll on indigenous forest dwellers, as well as on forest and savannah vegetation and biological diversity.

As food production must increase more than 75 per cent over the next 30 years, most of the gains will have to be achieved by obtaining higher yields from land that is already being farmed.

Achieving gains of that magnitude will require widespread adoption of thee technologies that today allow research stations to reap twice as much as farmers average. But steps must also be taken to avoid the social and environmental damage caused by a wholesale shift to monoculture production. A new green revolution will need to combine modern revolution will need to combine modern technology, traditional knowledge and an emphasis on farming, social and agro-ecological systems as well as yields.

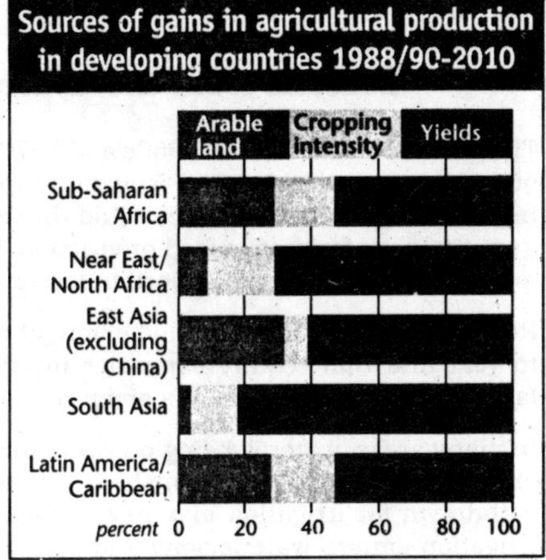

Achievements of the Green Revolution

Beginning in the 1960s, improved, high-yielding varieties of wheat spread quickly across Asia, soon followed by new strains of rice. Within 20 years, almost half of the wheat and rice land in developing countries was being sown with the new varieties. In Asia, where the impact of the green revolution was greatest, almost 90 per cent of wheat fields were planted with modern varieties and plantings of high-yielding rice had increased from 12 to 67 per cent.

In order to reap the potential of the new seeds, farmers also rapidly increased their use of mineral fertilizers, pesticides and irrigation. Between 1970 and 1990, fertilizer applications in developing countries shot up by 360 percent while pesticide use increased by 7 to 8 percent per year. The amount of land under irrigation increased by one-third. The gains in production were dramatic: world cereal yields jumped from 1.4 tonnes per hectare in the early 1960s to 2.7 tonnes per hectare in 1889-91. Over the past 30 years, the volume of world agriculture production has doubled and world agricultural trade has increased threefold.

These rapid gains helped avert a major food crisis in Asia and provided the springboard for rapid economic growth in China, southeast Asia and South Asia.

Lessons from the Green Revolution

The green revolution of the 1960s and 1970s depended on applications of fertilizers, pesticides and irrigation to create conditions in which high yielding modern varieties could thrive. It provided the basis for a quantum leap forward in food production. But it also taught scientists and policy-makers some important lessons for the future.

Reliance on seeds that have to be bought rather than saved from year to year and that require expensive inputs may exclude many poor farmers from the benefits of a green revolution.

In many areas, water is being pumped out of the ground for irrigation faster than it can be replenished. Up to 60 per cent of the water withdrawn for irrigation may never reach the crop. Poorly managed irrigation causes waterlogging and salt buildup that can turn fertile fields into a wasteland. Salinity now affects more than 20 per cent of the irrigated land in China and Pakistan.

Widespread use of just a few high-yielding varieties of wheat and rice may lead to the loss of traditional varieties and increase vulnerability to pests and diseases. By the end of this century, as few as 12 varieties of rice may cover 75 per cent of the fields in India.

The environmental damage caused by misuse of fertilizers and pesticides sometimes outweighs their advantages. Experts estimate that only about half of the fertilizer used may be actually benefit the crops; the remainder is lost from the soil by leaching run-off and volatilization. Similarly, a large percentage of pesticides may not reach target pests. Instead, they contaminate people, land, water and air, and foster the resistance strains of pests.

To achieve sustainable advances and minimize negative side effects, a new green revolution must also invest in education, farm, management, information and training.

Ingredients of a Green Revolution

The new green revolution draws on the best of the technologies that have doubled production over the past 30 years. At the same time, it emphasizes alternative approaches and improved farm management and information systems in order to minimize environmental damage from external inputs and benefit poor farmers and marginal areas bypassed by the original green revolution.

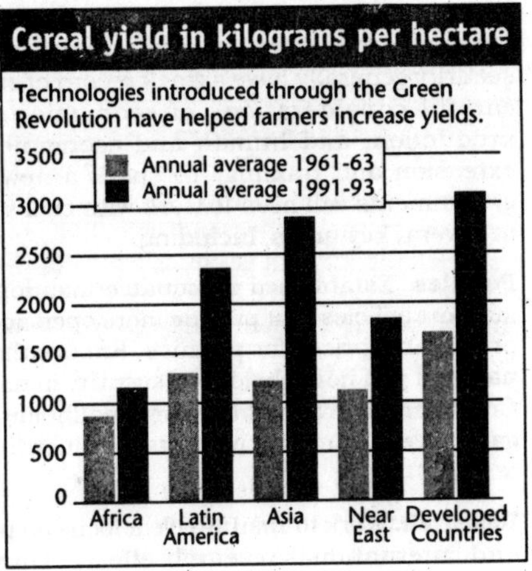

Examples of such approaches include:

- breeding of crop varieties that can withstand adverse conditions, such as salt-tolerant rice or more drought-resistant sorghums and millets;
- Soil nutrient cycling, through crop rotation and biomass recycling;
- reliance on genetic pest and disease resistance to replace or reduce chemical and mechanical pest control;
- Integrated crop management strategies to control pests and diseases and maintain soil fertility.

Increasing food production in the better endows areas can reduce pressures for expansion into marginal and more easily degraded lands.

Much attention must also be given to less fertile areas, where many of the poor and undernourished live. Here, a new green revolution must create more productive farming systems, including mixed crop-livestock systems that blend farmers' traditional techniques with new knowledge in crop and animal husbandry.

The Role of Government

Countries that have achieved greater national and household food security generally have a track record of strong support to agriculture, careful considerations of economic incentives for agricultural production, and human and economic investments in research, extension and training. To spark a new green revolution, national governments will need to work with civil society and the private sector in several key areas, including:

Policies: Established reasonable taxation systems, decentralize and support policies that provide more open access to markets and fair and predictable prices for produce. Ensure that a high priority is given to national and household food security in national development policies. Create an environment where smallholders, particularly women, can gain access to credit, markets and institutions and have secure land tenure.

Research: Work to ensure a clear focus on poverty alleviation in national and international research efforts. Give priority in research and investment to applications such as biological pest and weed control and IPM that can give higher and environmentally sustainable yields at lower cost, as well as to methods adapted to vulnerable and marginal areas. Agricultural research tends to be dwarfed by other priorities. The United States budget for 1996, for example, included research allocations of $35 billion for defense, $14 billion for space and $12 billion for health, but only $1.2 billion for agriculture.

Extension : Improve extension service, training and research facilities, including national universities, targeting efforts at those who do not have secure access to food. Studies have shown that extension can play a vital role in promoting new methods and technologies. Most countries allocate less than half the recommended 1 to 2 per cent of agricultural gross domestic product for extension. FAO has advised that some 1.25 million extension workers will be needed by the turn of the century, more than double the 600 000 in 1989.

Potential of a New Green Revolution

Typically dryland farmers obtain less than half the yields that research stations can achieve under similar conditions. In Andhra Pradesh, India, for example, research scientists have achieved impressive gains by double cropping grain and pulse.

Some rice farmers in Southeast Asia have recently neared research station yields. But further scientific advances could push yields higher. **The International Rice Institute aims to achieve annual yields of 15 tonnes per hectare, compared with the current world average of 3.5 tonnes.**

Substantial gains could also be achieved in livestock and aquaculture production. In tropical aquaculture, genetic improvements in carp and tilapia have led to yield gains of up to 50 per cent at the farm level over the past five years, offering hope for available and affordable protein.

If average annual farm yields per hectare could approach two-thirds of research station yields under comparable climatic conditions, enough food would be available to feed the hungry millions of tomorrow.

6

AQUACULTURE OFFERS CAUSE FOR HOPE

People have been farming fish for thousands of years. But today aquaculture has become big business in Asia, Latin America, North America, Europe. In 1994, world aquaculture production was worth US$39,000 million. Whether in large ponds, sea cages or tiny backyard ponds, aquaculture holds much promise for meeting increasing food demands. In fact, with most capture fisheries in decline, aquaculture is the best way to maintain and increase supplies of marine and freshwater fish.

Aquaculture for Food and Profit

Aquaculture, the farming of aquatic animals and plants, provides important economic and nutritional benefits to many regions of the developing world. In fact, aquaculture is overwhelmingly concentrated in the developing world, which accounts for more than 85 per cent of output by volume and 71 per cent by value.

Exports of high-value species such as shrimp and prawns earn much-needed foreign currency for these countries. Most importantly for food security, the production, processing and sale of fish offer the prospects of improved local nutrition by providing a ready source of high-quality protein as well as giving an opportunity to generate income.

Small-scale farmers see aquaculture as a way of making their food supply more secure by spreading their risks: pests or drought may decimate their maize or rice but there will still be fish to eat or trade for other foods.

Aquaculture Facts

- In 1994, aquaculture supplied 12.1 million metric tonnes of high quality food for direct human consumption;
- More than 85 per cent of total world aquaculture production was produced within developing countries in 1994;
- In 1994, over 90 per cent of total aquaculture production was in Asia, with China and India as the two leading producers;
- Aquaculture production in Low-Income-Food-Deficit countries grew at a rate of 13 per cent per year between 1984 and 1994, more than five times the 2.2 percent annual growth rate in developed countries.

Aquaculture in Mixed Farming Systems

Low-input aquaculture in rural is geared to providing food and diversification of income for the rural farmer and his immediate family and is just one of many part-time agricultural activities. The fish maintain their own populations and feed on the natural productivity of small ponds supplemented by house-hold vegetable wastes and composts.

Taken by itself, this basic fish farming unit may not be economically viable but, when combined with the cultivation of cereal crops and vegetables, it can make a unique contribution to the economies and nutritional levels of rural communities. Invariably, the success of subsistence aquatic farming depends on location, which in turn depends on land ownership and available water resources.

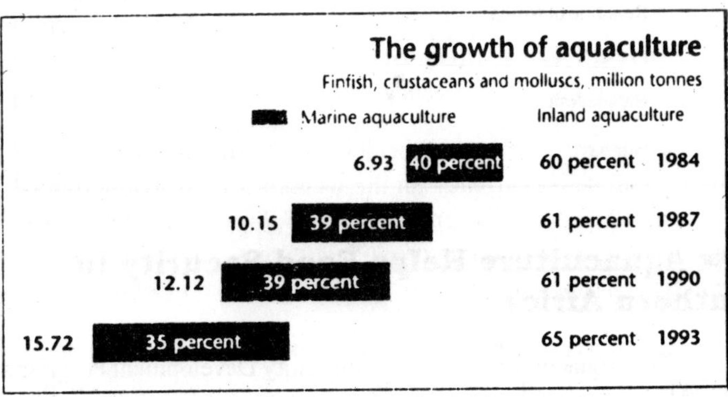

Aquaculture and the Environment

In spite of this promise, aquaculture projects are vulnerable to disease and environmental problems. Marine aquaculture is constrained by the rising pollution of coastal waters. Nutrient and organic over-enrichment, the accumulation of toxic chemicals, microbial contamination, siltation and sedimentation all jeopardize expansion. Where aquaculture results in the degradation of coastal mangroves, the breeding grounds of many wild species, it poses a major threat to biological diversity.

Better selection of production sites to safeguard the environment and sound management techniques can overcome most of these difficulties. Few environmental problems are experienced, however, with the low-input systems that make up the bulk of aquaculture.

Top Eleven Aquaculture Producers, 1994

	Tonnes
China	10 612 473
India	1 609 196
Japan	781 027
Indonesia	662427
United States	401 047
Thailand	519 373
Philippines	380 480
Republic of Korea	342 785
France	280 872
Bangladesh	269 560
Norway	218 124

How Aquaculture Helps Food Security in Southern Africa

The Aquaculture for local Community Development Programme (ALCOM) is a regional programme that operates in nine southern African countries. The programme aims to improve the standard of living of rural subsistence communities through aquaculture. The potential is considerable. For example, southern Africa has an estimated 20 000 small water bodies, most of them reservoirs built to provide water for domestic use, watering cattle and irrigating crops. In the past, some were stocked with fish but, lacking adequate management, their production remained low. They could yield an estimated 50 to 200 kg per hectare per year. Production is aided by warm water and plentiful food while nutrient-rich runoff promotes plankton growth. Aquaculture is sustainable because it does not reduce the water resource or conflict with most other uses.

Inland fisheries and aquaculture

The cultivation of **carp** has a long tradition, particularly in Europe and Asia. They still dominate aquaculture, accounting for most of the fish production. For home ponds they have the advantage of being non- carnivorous and so not requiring expensive protein-rich foods.

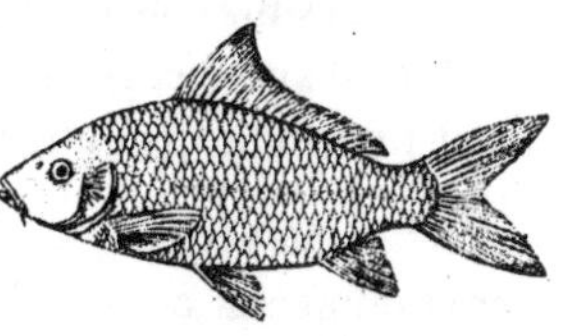

Tilapia, the mainstay of small-scale aquaculture for many poor farmers, have spread far from their original African home. Dubbed "the aquatic chicken" they are most widely farmed in Asia, particularly China, the Philippines and Thailand.

About half of the annual harvest of **shrimp** – a high value export product – comes from aquaculture. Progress in the production of shrimp over the past 10 years has been largely responsible for a fourfold increase in the annual harvest of crustaceans.

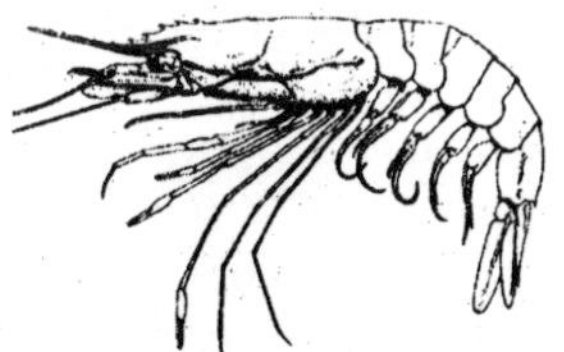

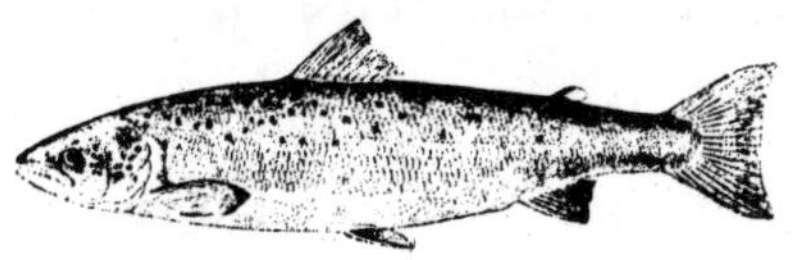

Culture of **salmon** in marine cages has been a high growth industry over the last decade, particularly in the cool temperate waters of Canada, Chile, and Australia.

ALCOM takes a new approach. It recognizes that rural farmers are only like to pursue fish farming on a part-time basis and therefore introduces aquaculture as an activity that complements existing farming systems and depends on little or no additional inputs.

Activities are broad-based and involve studies, investigations and pilot projects in the integration of aquaculture with farming systems and promotion of a wider role for women and youth in aquaculture development.

The future

It is difficult to assess the absolute growth potential of the aquaculture sub-sector, as it is more similar to agriculture than to fisheries. To attain 31 million tonnes of aquaculture production by 2010 will require a doubling of the estimated 1993 production in a period of 17 years. This seems feasible considering recent annual rates of expansion, the available technical knowledge, and the interest for the private sector, governments and financing institutions.

Nevertheless, the challenge is formidable. Proper planning, environmental considerations, proper system management and disease control will have to play a more important role than at present if crashes in production are to be avoided.

7

FORESTS AND NUTRITION

Trees and forests contribute in many ways to improving diets and combating hunger in local communities and rural households. They not only directly provide food and medicines; indirectly, they increase incomes and improve agricultural production, thereby improving access to food. Hunger and malnutrition would be significantly worse if it were not for the contribution of trees and forests to household food security.

Who Depends on Trees ?

Forests make a particularly important contribution to the nutrition of the rural poor, who, more than others, are likely to be dependent on trees for a significant part of their income and food supply. Forest-dwelling hunters and gatherers, the world's 300 million shifting cultivators and millions of smallholder and landless households living near forests, in the savannah or growing trees on their farms and compounds depend on trees as part of their survival strategies.

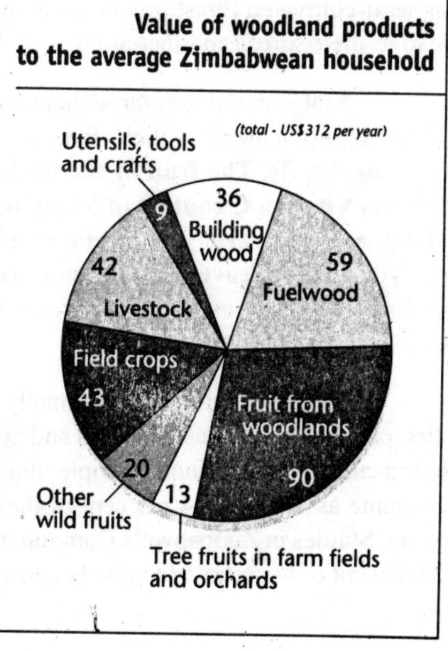

Forest foods can offer vital insurance against famine during times of seasonal food shortages or emergencies such as droughts, floods and wars. It is common for rural households to depend on forest foods between harvests when harvested stocks have been consumed but the next crops have still to mature. Women in particular count on these resources for supplementary nutrition, emergency foods, fuelwood for cooking and many other important products they need to ensure the nutritional well-being of their families.

One of the main contribution of forests and trees to household nutritional standards is as income. This income may be used to buy staple foods that usually cannot be produced in large quantities in the home garden. **In Peru, a hare hunter can earn the equivalent of US$1 350 a month, compared with a labourer's typical wage of $100.**

Food from Trees and Forests

Nearly every one consumes the tree foods in one form or another. Innumerable cultivated trees produced food : fruit and nut trees, coconut palms, plantains, olives and so on. Among the forest fruits that have gained popularity on the world market are avocados, mangos and guavas. Market forces have galvanized production of these fruits - formerly wild or semi-cultivated forest products - in their countries of origin and have lead to their spread to other areas.

Many households throughout the world grow trees in their home gardens, supplementing their diets with fruits, nut, edible leaves and other foodstuffs. **The fruit of the baobab far surpasses the orange's famous Vitamin C content of 57 mg per 100 g of fruit at 360 mg per 100 g, and one variety of jujube reaches levels as high as 1 000 mg per 100 g. Wild leaves contain more riboflavin than eggs, milk, nuts or fish**. In Ghana, over 100 wild plant species are valued for their and over 200 for their fruit.

Forests foods are traditionally used to supplement the staple diet, providing vitamins, minerals and proteins that are lacking in starch-based cultivated crop foods. People living near forest reserves in Nigeria consume as much as 84 per cent of their animal protein in the form of game. Studies in Zimbabwe's Communal Areas suggested that well over 90 percent of households routinely consume insect protein, mostly in the form of termites. Trees such as coconut and palm provide oils that are essential for cooking and numerous other household uses. Mushrooms and truffles are a source of protein, minerals and variety in diets.

Food from the Wild

Some of the many examples of tree food are:

- The nutritious fruit of the **mango:** the fruit matures during the "hunger season" and is an important supplement to the diets of people (especially children) living throughout the tropics.
- The nuts of the **sheanut** tree: a kind of butter is extracted from these nuts. which is used both for cooking and cosmetics.
- The vitamin-rich leaves. fruit and roots of the **baobob:** the leaves are used for preparing sauces. the fruit is an important source of vitamin C and the roots are consumed as an emergency food in times of drought.
- The fruit of the **oil palm:** it is used as a vegetable. for making sauces and for producing two different types of oil.
- The **Babassu palm:** the kernel of this palm is used to produce oil. its sap is used to make wine and the fruit is eaten both by humans and by wild animals that are commonly hunted for food. About 450 000 families in northern Brazil - some 2 million people - depend on the babassu for a significant part of their food and income.
- The myriad species of edible wild **mammles, reptiles, birds and insects** living in forests or trees. as well as the fish and shellfish from mangrove forests: these aquatic species account for up to 85 percent of the protein intake of people living near forests.
- **Giant snails** (*Achatina achatina* species): these are an important source of protein of Côte d'Ivoire and their shells provide calcium for animal feed and crop fertilization.
- The **sago palm:** it is a source of staple food for more than 300 000 people in Melanesia and is used regularly by 1 million more people across the globe. The starch from this palm is an important energy source.

Health for Humans, Animals and Plants

Many trees produce chemicals to protect themselves from the natural predators. These chemicals often have medicinal properties that are critical in maintaining levels of family nutrition. For example, the bark of the *Khaya senegalensis* is used for intestinal problems in tropical Africa, while the Copaiba tree of the Latin American tropics produces a substance used as an expectorant. Just one variety of yam, found in Mexico, provides the chemical that is the basis of virtually all oral contraceptives. **Folk medicine, which relies heavily on plants and the traditional knowledge about them, is the standard source of medical treatment for at least three-quarters of the world's people; some analysts set the figure as high as 90 per cent.** India has more than 2000 known medicinal plants, Malaysia around 1 000 and Brazil at least 3000.

Forests products provide important remedies for animal diseases, helping to safeguard livestock production. The hardiness and resistance or tolerance to disease and pests of many cultivated crops also depend on biological diversity - the key to improves crop varieties and animal breeds. Woods and forests, particularly in the tropics, are rich depositories of biological diversity.

Forest Ecosystems

In addition to their direct contribution to food supplies, trees provide habitats for animals, insects and plants that indirectly contribute to human nutrition. **Mangrove forests, which cover only about 1 600 Km², are essential to the life cycles of many of the world's major commercial fish species.** Shrimp, oysters, crabs and countless other edible species of aquatic animals also feed and breed in these forest ecosystems.

Besides being consumed directly, insects contribute to human diets in a number of ways. Honey is universally valued for its high energy content - more than 280 calories per 100 g. The blossoms of forests trees and plants growing below the forest canopy provide a year-round supply of food for bees in the form of nectar and pollen. In India, village-level bee-keeping yields an estimated 37 000 tonnes of honey a year. Similar products extracted directly from trees include sweeteners such as maple syrup and various sugar substitutes.

Building on Trees

Governments and forestry institutions can greatly improve the food security of small farmers and the rural poor through the creation of forest policies and forestry institutions that will support the needs of households that depend on trees for a significant part of their nutrition. Local communities need to be able to use forest lands and gather forest products without taxing the environment.

Sustainable agro forestry and tree crop programmes offer numerous strategies that can increase the already large contribution of trees and forests to food production and nutritional well-being. The effective integration of forests into development schemes can help to build on their value, improving nutrition worldwide

8

WOMEN FEED THE WORLD

Women play a decisive role in household and national food security. In rural areas - home to the majority of the world's hungry - they grow most of the crops for domestic consumption and are primarily responsible for preparing, storing and processing food. They also handle livestock, gather food, fodder and fuelwood and manage the domestic water supply. In addition, they provide most of the labour for post-harvest activities. Yet women's work often goes unrecognized, and they lack the leverage necessary to gain access to resource, training and finance.

How Women Influence Food Security

On a global scale women produce more than half of all the food that is grown. In sub-Saharan Africa and the Caribbean, they produce up to 80 per cent of basic foodstuffs. In Asia, they provide from 50 to 90 per cent of the labour for rice cultivation. And in Southeast Asia and the pacific as well as Latin America, women's home gardens represent some of the most complex agricultural systems known.

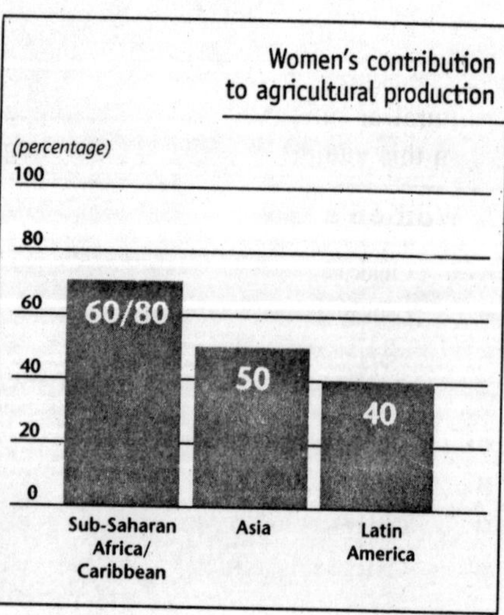

Women in the rural areas are almost exclusively responsible for the nutrition of their children, from gestation through weaning and throughout the critical period of growth. In addition, they are the principal food producers and prepares for the rest of the family. In general, most of this food comes from home gardens or from family and community plots. But it has been found that women also spend a significant part of their household income - a much larger proportionately than men - on buying additional food for the family.

Food preparation involves work far beyond caring for crops and livestock. Women must gather the wood for fires and carry the water they need for cooking and processing food. In many regions of the world, women spend up to five hours per day collecting fuelwood and water and upto four hours preparing food. In addition, rural women provide most of the labour for farming, from soil preparation to harvest. After the harvest, they are responsible for operations such as storage, handling, stocking, marketing and processing.

As more and more men migrate from rural areas in search of work, women bear a heavier burden. **In some regions of Africa, 60 percent of households are now headed by women.** The expanded workload can prompt women to cultivate less labour-intensive - though less nutritious - crops and to use agricultural practices that may harm the environment.

Women also pay a crucial role as custodians of genetic diversity and related knowledge on varieties and their uses, be it for food, medicine or cultural or other applications. From generation to generation, they pass on this vital knowledge to their daughters.

A Women's Work is Never Done

- Childcare
- Gathering Wood
- Carrying Water
- Cooking Food
- Processing Food
- Marketing Crops
- Caring for Crops
- Caring for Animals
- Weaving, Crafts

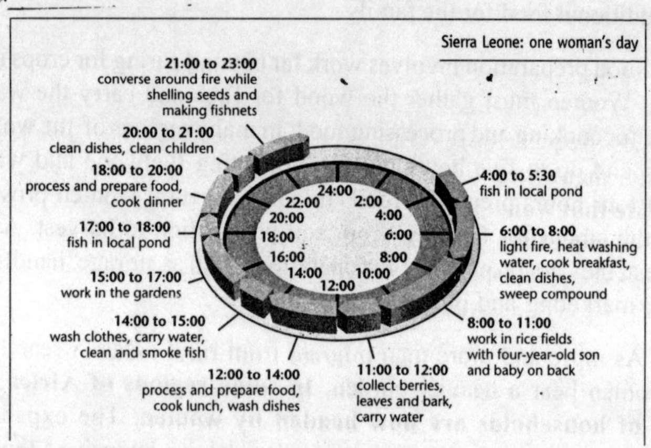

Invisibility and Gender Bias

Despite their contribution to food security, women tend to be "invisible" actors in development. As a result, their contribution is poorly understood and often underestimated. There are many reasons for this. Work in the household is considered to be a part of woman's duties as wife and mother, rather than an occupation to be accounted for in the national economy. Outside of the house-hold, a great deal of rural women's labour - whether regular or seasonal - goes unpaid and is, therefore , rarely taken into account in official statistics. In most of the countries, women do not own the land they cultivate. When land is owned by women, it tends to be smaller, less valuable plots that are also overlooked in statistics. Furthermore, women are usually responsible for the food crops destined for immediate consumption by the household, that is, for subsistence crops rather than cash crops. Also, when data is collected for national statistics, gender is often ignored or the data is biased in the sense that is collected only from males, who are assumed to be the heads of households.

Rural women's invisibility is further accentuated by their lack of political power and social representation resulting from prevailing attitudes, gender-biased legal and social structures and illiteracy, among other factors. Extension services reach women much less frequently than they do men. **Statistics indicate that women receive no more than 5 per cent extension resources.** This lack of knowledge often hinders the progress of women and their contribution to food security, particularly at the family level.

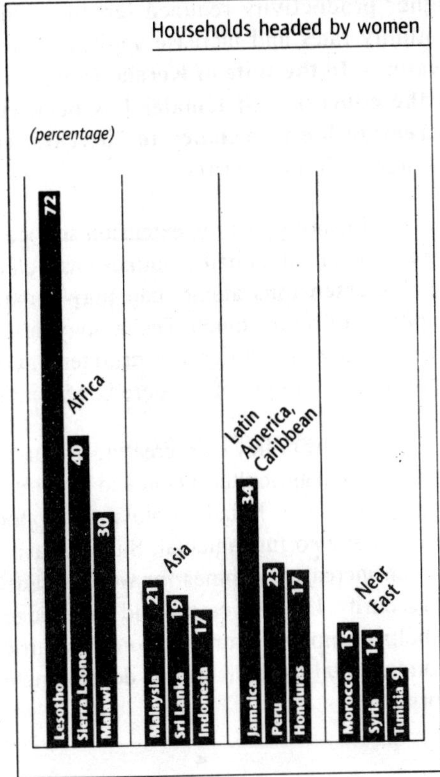

The combined effect of these handicaps is an increasing feminization of poverty. **Since the 1970s, the number of women living below the poverty line has increased by 50 per cent, in comparison with 30 per cent for their male counterparts. More than 70 per cent of the 1300 million poor people today are women.**

Improving Food Security by Empowering Women

Education can play a major role in improving the status of women, the nutrition of their families and national food production. **A cost-benefit analysis carried out by the World Bank indicates that investment in the education of females has the highest rate of return of any possible type of investment in developing nations.** It results in higher productivity reduced fertility, reduced child morbidity and mortality rates and increase application of environmental protection measures. **In the state of Kerela, India, a long standing commitment to the education of females has been cited as a major factor in increasing life expectancy to 70 years, compared with the Indian average of 56 to 58 years.**

Ensuring that the extension services address the specific needs of women - and their daily routines - as well as the development of more females extensions agents can play a major role in improving the conditions of rural women. Technology designed to suit women's needs can contribute to mitigating drudgery and provide women with an opportunity to join in other more beneficial or rewarding activities.

On the policy side, creating a situation that allows women more access to good agricultural land and resources, including farm inputs, as an important step. Equal employment opportunities - and competitive wages - are also fundamental. Studies have shown a direct correlation between increased incomes for women and improvement in household food security. Lastly access to and knowledge of credit and legal systems can help to empower women. Women's participation in decision-making is fundamental to their role in development and contribution to food security.

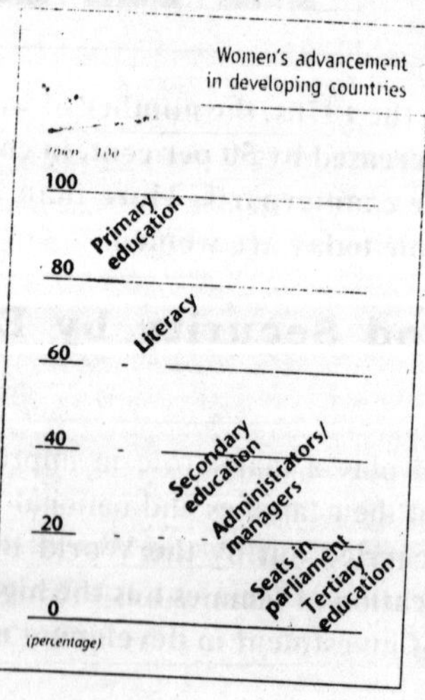

9

WATER AND FOOD SECURITY

In many countries, water scarcity represents a critical constraint to food production and a major cause of poverty and hunger. Improved water management is one of the keys to producing enough food to alleviate the suffering of today and feed an additional 3,000 million people by the year 2030.

Water: Growing Demand, Limited Resources

Water Resources, until recently considered cheap and plentiful, are now recognized to be scarce and valuable. **More than 230 million people live in 26 countries classified as "water deficient", 11 of which are in Africa**. And a number of countries facing severe water shortages is likely to increase dramatically in the next decade.

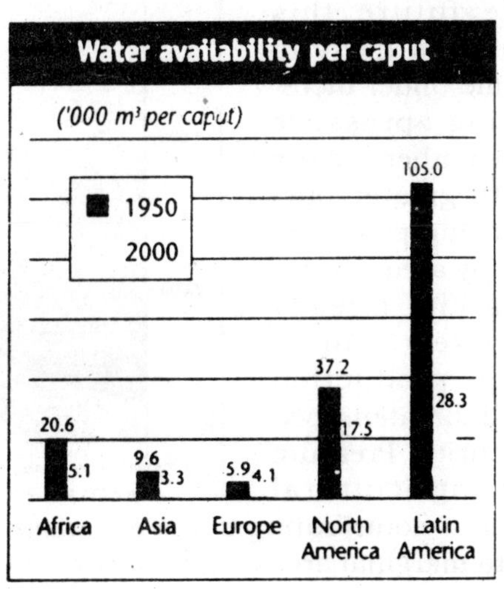

By the year 2000, six out of seven East African Countries and all five North African countries bordering the Mediterranean will face acute water shortages. All the countries in North Africa, except Morocco, already import half or more of their grain.

Demand for water is escalating, contributing to intensified competition among users. In many areas, giving water to one user means denying it to another. In a world where available surface fresh-water resources are extremely unevenly distributed, this has the potential to provoke national, regional and international disputes.

Water as a Constraint to Food Production

Without investment in water, the prospects for improving food production and increase food security are remote.

Agriculture accounts for over two-thirds of the world's water withdrawal, yet in the future this share is likely to come under increasing pressure from other sectors with greater purchasing power. In many areas, water scarcity already severely limits food production and threatens food security. Pressure on agricultural land is contributing to the expansion of rainfed agriculture into marginal areas characterized by risky rainfall regimes.

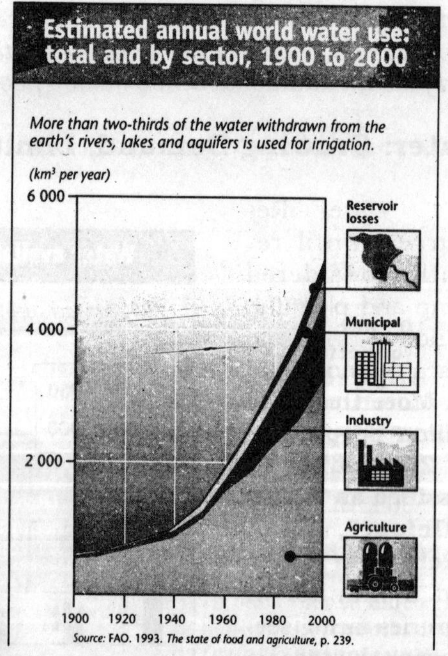

Source: FAO. 1993. The state of food and agriculture, p. 239.

This is forcing millions of impoverished people to undertake unsustainable farming systems in ecologically fragile areas.

To partly offset the variability of rainfall, farmers tend to select crops with the genetic capacity to withstand the risks of rainfall failure. Many poor farmers are reluctant to grow high-yielding varieties that require large amounts of water, since one crop failure can threaten the survival of their entire household.

Irrigation's Contribution

Irrigated land is more than twice as productive as rainfed cropland. Today, only 16 per cent of the world's croplands are irrigated, but those lands yield some 36 percent of the global harvest.

In the developing countries, irrigation increase yields for most crops by 100 to 400 per cent. Irrigation also allows farmers to reap the economic benefits of growing higher-level cash crops.

Half or even two-thirds of future gains in crop production are expected to come from irrigated land.

In the developing world, where about 20 percent arable land is irrigated, the prevalence of irrigation varies widely within and among countries and crops. Irrigation makes the greatest contribution to global food security in Asia. **Irrigated lands account for as much as 80 per cent of food production in Pakistan, some 70 per cent in China and over 50 per cent in India and Indonesia.**

In Africa, where only about 10 per cent of food production comes from irrigated lands FAO calculates that irrigation has been developed on only 30 per cent of 42.5 million hectares with irrigation potential.

A World Bank/UNDP study estimates that irrigation could be extended over an additional 110 million ha in developing countries, producing enough more grain to feed 1 500 to 2 000 million people.

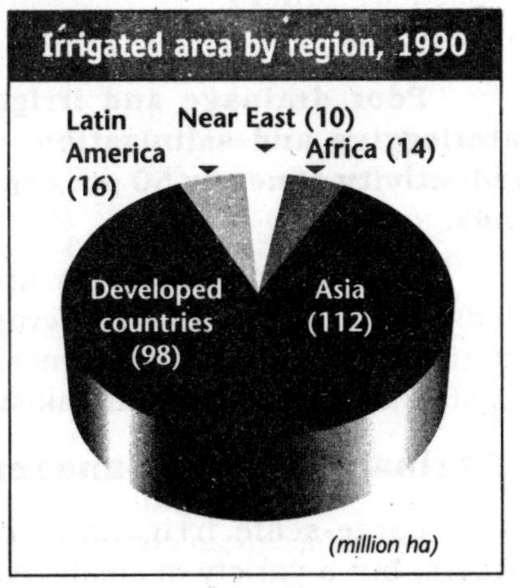

Poor Water Management: A Threat to Soil, Water and Food Security

Poorly managed irrigation contributes to water shortages and pollution, land degradation and the spread of waterborne diseases. In many regions, water is being pumped out of the ground for irrigation faster than it can be replenished. **Overpumping in India's Tamil Nadu state has lowered the water table by 25 to 30 m in a decade.** Much of this water is wasted. **As much as 60 percent of the water is withdrawn for irrigation often does not reach the crop**. It is through canal leakage, spillage, infiltration and unproductive evaporation, although some of this water reaches the river or groundwater, allowing it to be used by others downstream.

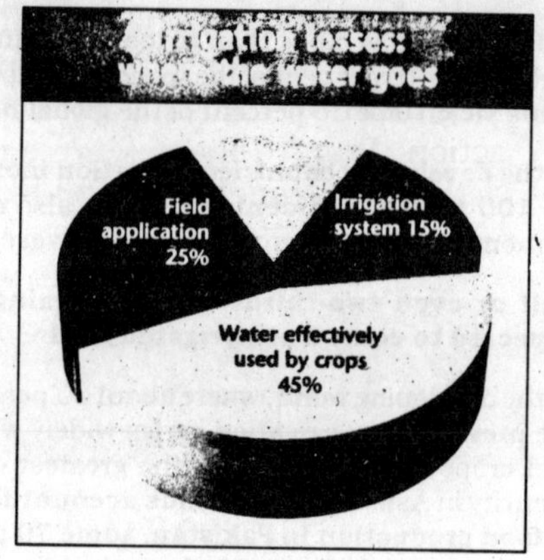

Poor drainage and irrigation practices lead to waterlogging and salinization, which have sapped the productivity of nearly 50 per cent of the world's irrigated lands.

Unless irrigated fields are drained properly, salt builds up in the soil as water evaporates, making the land infertile. Salinity now affects more than 20 per cent of the irrigated land in China and Pakistan.

Sustainable Water Management

Large-scale irrigation projects are beyond poor farmers, but a variety of small-scale, affordable techniques can increase food production. Examples include:

Water Harvesting. Collecting runoff and using it to irrigate crops, pastures and trees can significantly improve both yields and the reliability of agriculture production. Experience in Burkina Faso, the Sudan and Kenya shows that rain harvested from one hectare for supplementary irrigation of an other can triple or even quardruple production.

Low-lift Pumps. Cheap, dependable motors and pumps, along with increasing availability of fuel, have revolutionized irrigation. Small pump schemes, individual and communal, have begun to play an important role in augmenting food production. Pump schemes are easy to operate. They also provide indirect benefits by linking water for domestic use to irrigation.

Treadle pumps. Simple, inexpensive walking pumps have enabled poor farmers in many Asian countries to increase their incomes and production by allowing a second crop to be harvested during the dry season, new varieties of vegetables to be planted and crops to be grown in semi-arid areas. These pumps are often operated by women, who also use them to obtain drinking water.

Water Management in Africa

FAO recently estimated the potential for using water in agriculture on the basis of soil, climate and water conditions. The results confirmed that irrigation is far from being the only source of agricultural water control in Africa. A Huge untapped potential remains available for water harvesting and agricultural management of lowland and valley bottoms.

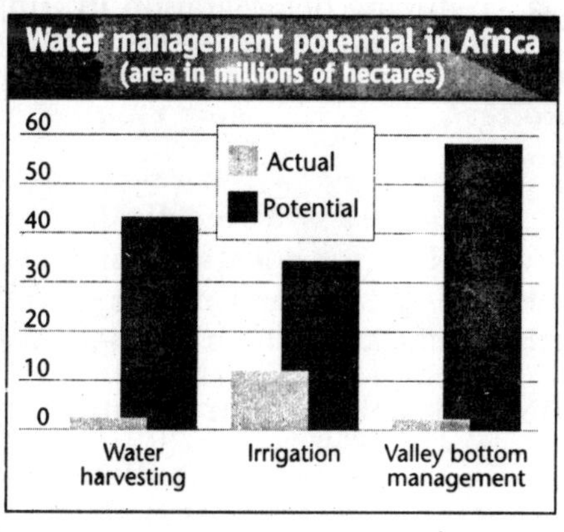

Towards a Water-Centered Strategy for Food Production

Improved water management holds the key to increasing food production through use of high-yielding varieties and improved cultural practices. Global targets by the year 2010 are:

- to increase water-use efficiency by at least 20 per cent
- to open an additional 40 million hectares of land to irrigation
- to reclaim 10 million hectares of waterlogged and salinized lands.

Key steps toward achieving these goals include:

- assessing the potential of national soil and water resources to increase food production
- promoting sustainable, efficient and socially equitable use of water
- adopting a river-basin approach as the first option in all water development
- integrating technical and social research to develop low-cost, small-scale, distributed technology that responds to farmers' needs
- increasing investment in water infrastructure as an integral part of wide-ranging area development programmes
- reducing deforestation in upper catchments to reduce floods and erosion.

10

LIVESTOCK AND FOOD SECURITY

Livestock play important roles in farming systems in developing countries, helping provide food and income, drought power, fertilizer and soil conditioner, household energy and a means of disposing of otherwise unwanted crop residues. It is a major industry: 12 percent of the world's population depends solely on livestock for its livelihood.

Livestock for Food

Livestock make an important contribution to the food supplies of developing countries. Furthermore, production of livestock products in increasing fast. Over the past 20 years, cereal production in developing countries has increased by 78 per cent and fish production by 113 per cent while meat production has risen by 127 per cent and egg production by 331 per cent. The fastest increases in meat production have been poultry and pigs.

Even so, many people in developing countries cannot afford animal products, as a result of which per caput consumption of meat is only 17.7 kg/year, compared to 81.6 kg/year in developed countries. About 60 per cent of dietry protein is from animal products in developed countries, compared to only 22 percent in developing countries. There is, therefore, substantial room for expansion of livestock production.

Further expansion of livestock production could raise

problems in developing countries, but it is also true that animal products offer several advantages over crops. For example:

- meat and milk can be produced year-round, being less seasonal than cereals, fruit and vegetables;
- animals, particularly small ones, can be slaughtered as the need arises, for food or income; and
- both milk and meat can be preserved - milk as clarified butter, curd or cheese, and meat by drying, curing, smoking and salting.

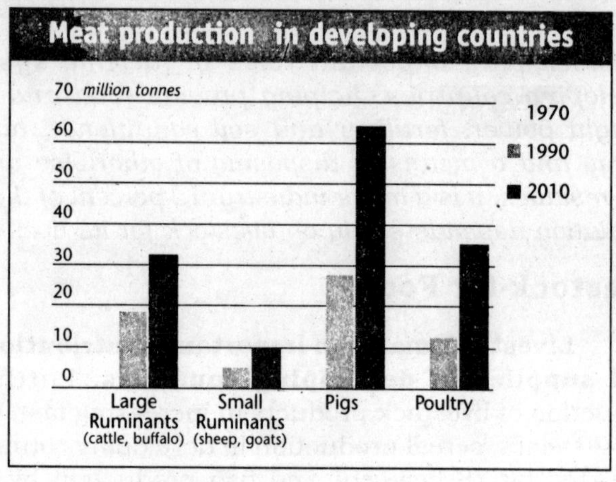

Income and the Economy

Livestock play an important role in the economy, both at the farm and national levels. For the farmers, they provide

- Liquid assets;
- a hedge against inflation;
- a means of reducing the risks associated with crops, when used in mixed farming systems;
- a source of extra income (rabbits, poultry and pigs) for landless households;
- a source of regular income from sales of milk and meat;

- a source of sporadic income from the sale of live animals, hides, wool and meat;
- draught power, transport and breeding services, for the farmer himself and to rent out; and
- opportunity to increase employment through on- and off-farm processing.

At the national level, increased production of livestock products will reduce the need for high-cost imports. With the reduction of milk subsidies in developed countries and the establishment of more realistic exchange rates, it is an appropriate time for an expansion of local dairy industries.

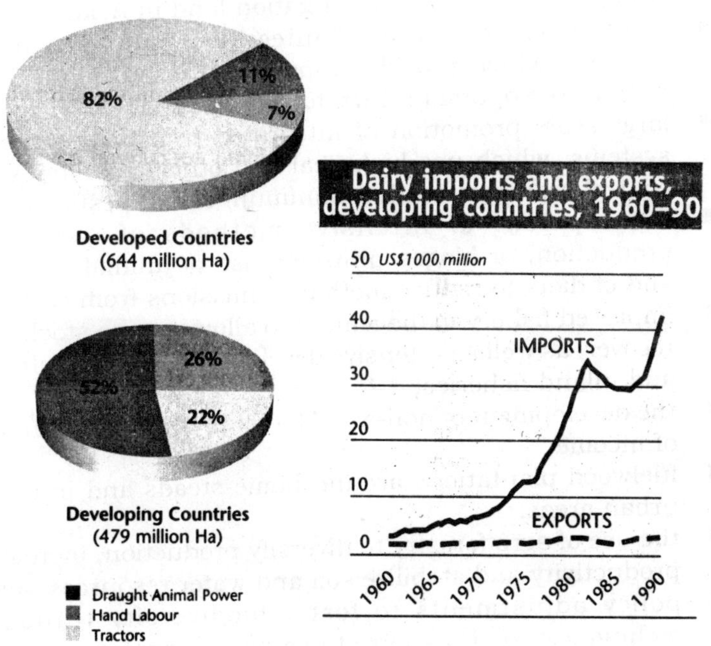

How to Reduce Environmental Impacts

Environmentally sound food production systems must achieve three aims: increase production and productivity, reduce pollution and resource degradation, and be socially and economically viable.

Among hundreds of attractive possibilities, the following will have the priority:

- the prevention of soil erosion with live hedges, grass strips, orchard trees, simple bench and ridge terraces, contour ploughing, strip cropping, limited tillage, green manuring, windbreaks and mulches;
- improving the management of irrigated areas, in particular by improving drainage to the 11 million hectares of waterlogging irrigation land in Asia;
- large-scale promotion of integrated plant nutrition systems, which provide crops with the nutrients they need at the optimal return to the farmer;
- large-scale promotion of integrated pest management systems, which use biological and other techniques to control crop pests with a minimum use of pesticides;
- development of intensive methods of livestock production, of biogas units for use of animal wastes, and of diets to reduce methane emissions from cattle;
- improved fishery management to allow marine stocks to recover, as well as intensive development of aquaculture and inland fisheries;
- the development of non-wood forest products as sources of income;
- fuelwood plantations around home-steads and in peri-urban areas;
- the use of agro forestry to diversify production, increase productivity and stabilize soil and water resources; and
- policy adjustments to foster biodiversity through techniques such as mixed use buffer zones to protect existing areas, and the maintenance of crop diversity through crop rotation and sequences.

The Role of Government

Unlike many other sectors, governments have a special role to play in promoting rural development and environmentally sound agriculture. Governments should:

- Support environmentally-based practices through incentives that promote the efficient use of inputs and encourage the full use of human resources
- reduce subsidies that lead to adverse environmental impacts
- introduce water pricing policies and institutional changes to increase the efficiency of water use in all sectors
- develop policies to promote the best land-use practices and the equitable distribution of resources
- transform smallholder agriculture into modern, competitive and productive enterprises by investing in sustainable agricultural and rural development
- asses food production potential in and around cities, and produce more food near to where it is consumed
- improve infrastructure so that farmers can deploy quality seed, fertilizers and equipment, and equip extension staff to promote sound environmental management practices.

Securing Food within Nature's Limits

Scientists believe that technical options are available to provide enough food for future populations without harming the environment.

Keys to achieving this in practice will be:

- **The Efficient Use of Resources** - that is, converting scarce resources into useful products in a way that is economically viable but that minimizes impact on the environment during production, processing and marketing;
- **The use of Planning and Implementation Frameworks** to facilitate and diffuse the response provided by science and technology to the demand for more food.

- **An Approach to Governance** that promotes dialogue with diverse interest groups and shares decision-making authority and control over allocation of resources to district and local levels, while simultaneously discouraging corrupt or inefficient practices.

The political and administrative framework for achieving these goals should have at least four main elements.

- **Introduction of Ecologically-Sound, Participatory Land-use Planning** to identify and mitigate the environmental impacts of increased food production;
- **Social and Economic Policies** that encourage food producers to manage their soil fertility and moisture, pest populations and biological diversity through integrated management systems. In many cases, success will depend on first addressing social or economic constraints such as equitable land tenure and access to capital, unemployment and the marginalization of women;
- **Investment in Human Capital and Rural Infrastructure** by integrating agriculture research, education and extension and training agriculture advisors to help farmers apply environmentally-sound food production methods;
- **Continuous environmental assessment, monitoring and evaluation** of the impacts of food production practices, and feeding this information back to policy-makers and producers.

11

AGRICULTURE AND FOOD SECURITY

Global food production has grown rapidly over the past 30 years, managing to outstrip population growth. Yet today, in a world that can produce enough food to supply an adequate diet for all, hundreds of millions of people go hungry. Chronic undernutrition persists mainly in countries with low incomes, most of which depend heavily on agriculture. So long as that is the case, eliminating hunger will require concerted efforts to accelerate agriculture and rural development in those countries.

The Situation Today - Hunger Amid Plenty

As Heads of State and government gather in Rome for the World Food Summit, they can look with satisfaction on the progress that has been made in increasing food production and food security, with concern on the high levels of hunger and malnutrition that persist, and with dismay on the prospect that future progress will be slow and uneven.

After 30 years of rapid growth in agricultural production, **the world can produce enough food to provide every person with more than 2 700 calories per day** - a level which is normally sufficient to ensure that all have access to adequate food, provided distribution is not too unequal.

Yet more than 800 million people in the developing world suffer from chronic undernutrition.

Lack of essential energy and protein stunts the bodies, minds and hopes of some 200 million children.

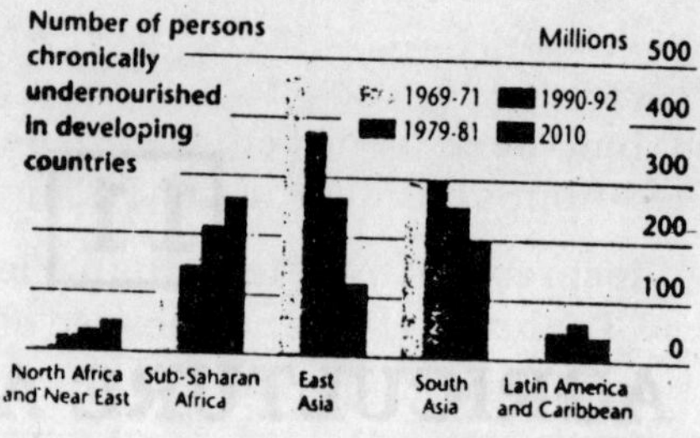

Over the past few years, world gain stocks have dwindled to dangerously low levels, highlighting the fragility of food supplies in a world where the population is expected to reach 7 billion people by the year 2010, almost double the 3.7 billion of 1970.

Achievements and Lessons of the Past

In the early 1960s, global food supplies for direct human consumption stood only 2 300 calories per person per day, very unequally distributed. In developed countries the average was already 3030 calories per day. In the developing world it languished below 2 000. **Probably more than half the people in the developing world suffered from chronic undernutrition.**

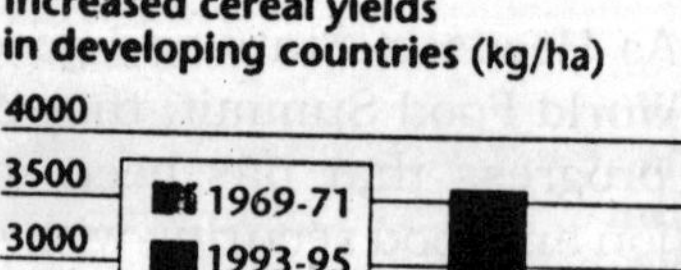

Then over 30 years, the world population more than doubled. But agricultural production increased even faster. **By 1994, global food supplies for human consumption had climbed to 2 710 calories per person per day. And the percentage of chronically undernourished people in the developing world had been reduced to 20 per cent.** These gains resulted from a number of factors including:

- **Widespread Use of New, High-Yielding Crop Varieties and Technologies.** The package of technologies referred to as the green revolution, including increased use of

Progress for Some But Not For All

Despite gains in food production and food security on a world scale, many countries and whole regions failed to make progress in recent decades.

Sub-Saharan Africa produces less food per person today than it did 30 years ago. The number of chronically under nourished people in the region has more than double since 1970, from 96 million to over 200 million.

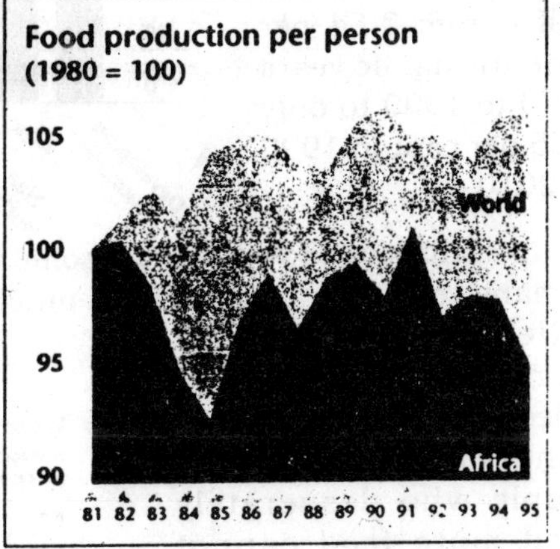

For the most part, countries endowed with better resources to begin with scored rapid gains in production. On the other hand, yields generally stagnated in those countries that started with very low yields. **Wheat yields in the ten most productive countries jumped from 2.65 to 5.12 tonnes per hectare. But average yields among countries at the other end of the scale edged up only from 0.47 to 0.76 tonnes per hectare.**

After achieving significant growth in per caput food production during the 1960s, numerous developing countries failed to make progress over the past two decades. The majority of them registered outright declines between 1972 and 1992.

irrigation, fertilizer and pesticides, increased yields for millions of farmers, although with some negative social and environmental impacts.

- **Increased Reliance on Food Imports**. During the 1970s alone, net imports of cereals by developing countries more than tripled - from 20 million to 67 million tonnes.

Sources of Hope ... Grounds for Concern

While agricultural production will grow faster than world population over the coming decades, the margin will continue to shrink. The annual increase in production per person will be cut in half - from 0.54 per cent during the years 1970 to 1990 to only 0.25 per cent in 1990 to 2010.

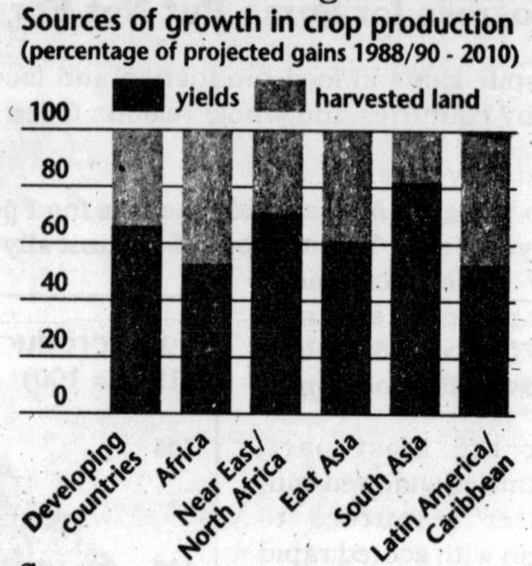

This slow-down reflects some positive trends. People in many countries already eat as much as they want, leaving little room for further increases. But it also reflects the grim reality that hundreds of millions of people who desperately need more food cannot afford to buy it at prices that would stimulate increased production.

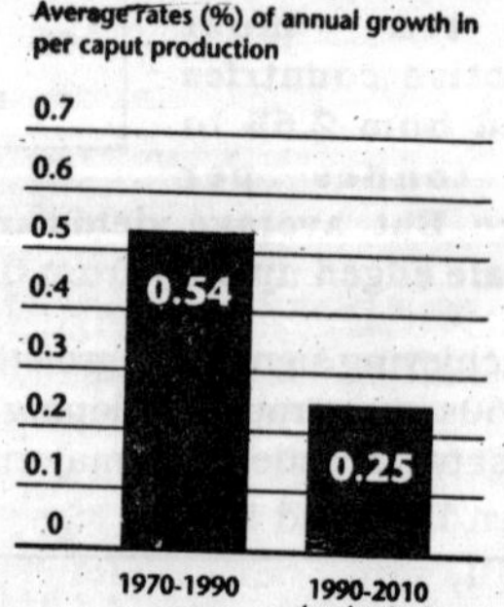

Most of the projected gains in production will come from more intensive agriculture and increased yields, rather than from farming new lands.

Looking Forward - Continued Gain, Continued Pain

Looking ahead to the year 2010, world agricultural growth is expected to slow but should still outpace population growth. As a result, **food availability in the developing countries will improve to an average above 2 700 Calories per person per day.**

But not all regions and countries will share equally in these gains in production and nutrition. The situation in Africa south of the Sahara will deteriorate further, while progress in south Asia will be painfully slow.

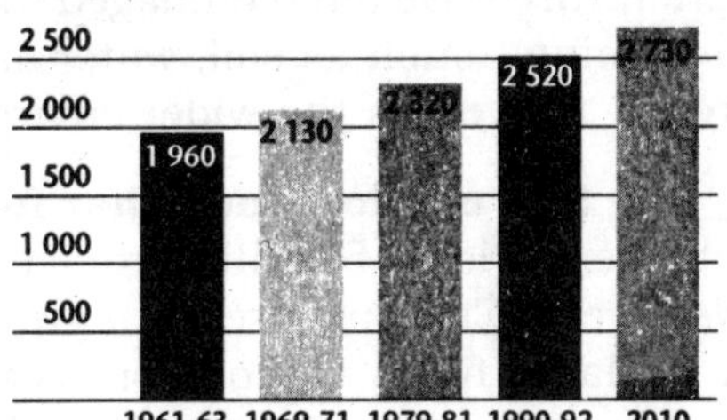

By the year 2010, the number of chronically undernourished people in sub-saharan Africa may still be some 264 million, or 30 per cent of the population.

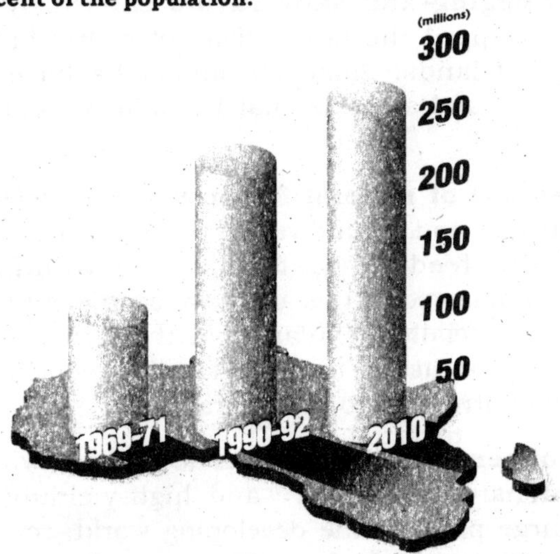

Overall, some 680 million people may still suffer from chronic undernutrition in 2010 - only a small decline from today - although they will represent a smaller percentage of the total population.

Although significant reserves of potential agricultural land can be identified at a global level, much of this is concentrated in a few countries or is only marginally suitable for crop production.

Developing countries will depend even more heavily on food imports. Net imports are likely to increase to more than 160 million tonnes tonnes by the year 2010.

Environmental Constraints

In the past, expansion and intensification of agriculture have often damaged the very resources essential to farming - such as soil, water and the genetic diversity of crops - as well as the wider environment.

Soil erosion and other forms of land degradation rob the world of 5 million to 7 million ha of farming land every year. Clearing forests or growing crops on steep slopes or on large fields without protection against the wind can lead to erosion.

Waterlogging and salinization caused by poor drainage have sapped the productivity of nearly half the world's irrigated lands. Some 30 million ha have been severely damaged and an additional 1.5 million ha are lost each year.

Excess use of mineral fertilizers and pesticides can pollute surface and groundwater sources. Nitrates from fertilizers and feedlot wastes have contaminated groundwater in many countries and have been identified as a health risk, especially for infants. At the same time, in some countries the use of too little fertilizer depletes soil nutrients and contributes to soil degradation.

Loss of genetic diversity has accelerated with the spread of intensive agriculture and high-yielding crop varieties to large parts of the developing world, replacing the traditional diversity of crops with monocultures.

Deforestation accelerated during the 1980s, with more than 15 million ha of tropical forests lost each year, mainly to provide land for agriculture.

Agriculture also contributes significantly to release of greenhouse gases that have been linked to global warming. Some 30 per cent of carbon dioxide emissions result from deforestation and other land use practices such as rangeland burning and agriculture may account for as much as 90 per cent of nitrous oxide emissions.

The challenge for the future will be simultaneously intensify production and minimize harm to the resources and the wider environment upon which present and future generations depend.

12

AGRICULTURAL RESEARCH AND FOOD SECURITY

Agricultural research has been one of the keys to increasing food production over the past half century at a rate that has outstripped rapid increase in population. As per person availability of arable land, water and other resources continues to shrink, further commitment and advances in research will be critical to ensure that future generations will be better fed, clothed and housed than they are today.

The Value of Agricultural Research

Agricultural research has been a major factor in increasing global food production by 80 per cent since mid-1960s, with more than a half of the increase in developing countries. As can be seen from the bar chart on page 67, yields of maize, rice and wheat more than doubled in many regions during the period 1960-94 as a result of the introduction of improved varieties, irrigation, fertilizers and improved crop management. Research advances have also contributed to food security by developing improved breeds and varieties of livestock, fish and trees to enhance livestock production, aquaculture, agroforestry and mixed farming systems. This has had a number of major effects on developing countries:

- increased and more stable supplies;
- declining national and international cereal prices;
- less reliance on food aid (between 1970 and 1990 food

aid as a percentage of total food consumption was reduced by 14 per cent);

- increased employment and income through agriculture-led economic growth; and
- decreased incidence of poverty.

Positive effects on the environment have included reduction in the use of marginal land for agriculture. Agricultural research has also reduced the need for fertilizers and pesticides as a result of integrated plant nutrition pest management.

Average yield of rice wheat and maize by region 1960 and 1994 (tonnes/hectare)

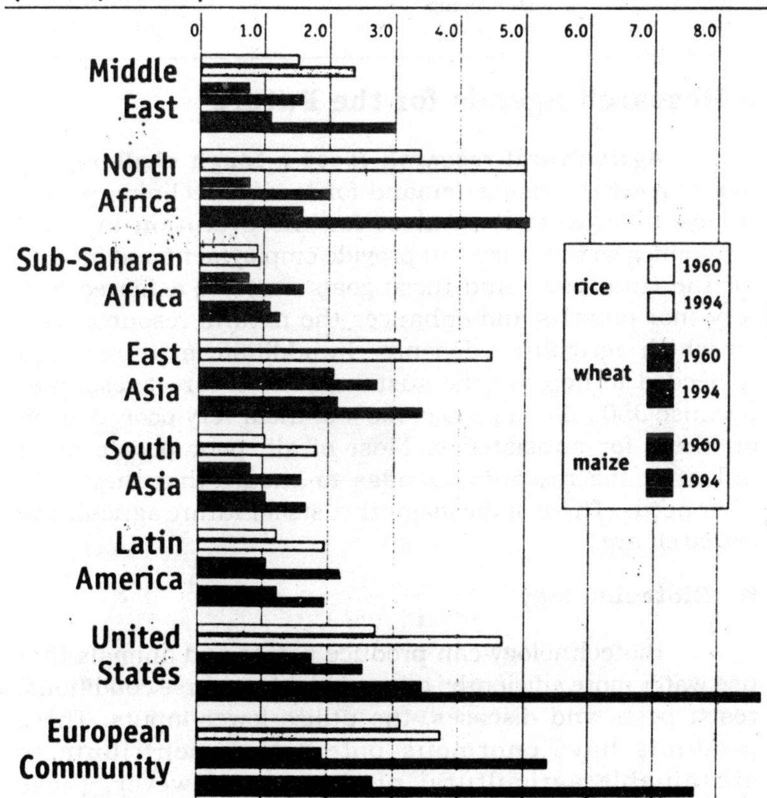

Returns on Agricultural Research

Commodity	*Country*	*Rates of Return (Percent)*
Maize	South America	191
Maize	Mexico	78-91
Rice	Indonesia	60-65
Rice	India	65
Soybeans	Brazil	46-69
Sugarcane	Philippines	51-71
Potatoes	Peru	22-42
Cowpeas	Senegal	60-80
Wheat	Pakistan	58
Wheat	Developing Countries	50

A Research Agenda for the Future

Agricultural research faces a tough challenge. It has to meet the rising demand for food at declining prices. It has to provide a catalyst for the evolution of rural economies so that they can provide employment and income for the rural poor. And these goals must be achieved in a way that protects and enhances the natural resource base on which agriculture depends. In addition, more research is needed to improve the sustainability of forest resources because 350 million people, most of them very poor, depend on them for subsistence. Most of all, poor people must influence the research agendas to ensure that they meet their needs. Three of the major thrusts for future agricultural research are :

■ Biotechnology

Biotechnology can produce plants and animals that use water more efficiently, grow in highly adverse conditions, resist pests and diseases, the utilize fewer inputs. These products have enormous potential to contribute to sustainable agricultural production. However, these organisms must be evolved with great attention to safety issues.

■ Natural Resource Management

Increase research is needed on the management of the natural resources on which agriculture depends - soil, water, plants and animals. More efficient management strategies are needed for both soil and water. Research is needed to improve irrigation and to improve technologies for the protection and conservation of both soil and water. In addition, the research agenda must address issues of appropriate technologies for the conservation, maintenance and utilization of the diversity of biological resources needed on the farm.

■ Policy Analysis

Policy research is desperately needed in most developing countries where decisions are too often guided by inadequate documentation and sufficient knowledge. Subjects that require investigation include inappropriate price policies that encourage inefficient use of inputs and that encourage unsustainable cropping systems. Policy research must also include a through understanding of decisions taken at the household level.

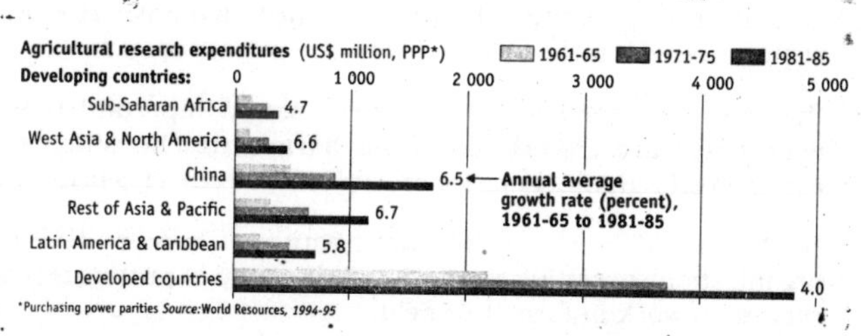

Finding the Funding

Investment in agricultural research grew fast during the 1960s and 1970s, more slowly in the 1980s and has been stagnant during the 1990s. In developing countries, the proportion of the total agricultural gross domestic product spent on research is about 0.5 per cent, compared to 2-4 per cent in developed countries.

Research investment must be increased now to meet the growing demand for food without price increase or deterioration of the agricultural resource base. To improve food security in a sustainable manner, developing countries will have to invest at least one per cent of their agricultural

Improving the Research System

The major components of the global agricultural research system are the National Agricultural Research Systems (NARS) of developed and developing countries and the International Agricultural Research Centres (IARCs).

In 1995, developed countries' NARS accounted for about 48 per cent of global research expenditure with about one-third of the scientists involved while developing country NARS accounted for the same proportion of research expenditure with nearly two-thirds of the scientists involved. The IARCs accounted for the balance of about 4 per cent of global research expenditure.

There are a number of ways in which this system can be improved:

- Correct the major weakness of the public sector NARS in developing countries which include lack of flexibility, susceptibility to political interference, lack of responsiveness to client demand and lack of funding. The current level of funding of 0.5 per cent of agricultural GDP should be raised to at least 1 per cent;
- agricultural universities should strengthen their links with public sector research institutes and with the private sector;
- the private sector will play an increasingly important role. As economies are transformed and agriculture becomes more commercialized, the scope for private sector research will increase;
- NARS should increase the participation of farmers and their organizations in setting research priorities and in putting research results to work in farmers's field;
- find new and innovative ways of enabling the components of the global agricultural system to work together to increase the efficiency and effectiveness of scarce financial resources; and
- improve the efficiency of research efforts in natural resource management, which traditionally falls outside the scope of agricultural research.

output in research over the short term and two per cent over the long term. Investment of this magnitude will not be forthcoming unless the global research system is improved in ways suggested in the box on the right.

The reward for transforming and investing further in agricultural research will have a thriving agricultural sector, a necessary condition for economic growth, providing food, income and employment to the poor, and improving resource conservation and environmental protection.

13

FISHERIES AND FOOD SECURITY

Fish are an important source of both food and income to many people in developing countries. While many capture fish stocks are already approaching their exploitation limits, there is considerable potential to expand aquaculture in order to improve food security.

Fish for Food and Income

Fish are a valuable and nutritious food. They contribute to people's well-being both because of the income they provide and because of the food they supply.

More than 120 million people are estimated to depend on fish for all or part of their incomes. Most are relatively poor. In Africa, as much as 5 per cent of the population, some 35 million people, depend wholly or partly on the fisheries sector for their livelihood.

Fish sales also provide important foreign exchange. Net exports by the less developed countries were worth more than US$20 000 million in 1994 - more than for coffee, banana, rubber, tea, meat or rice.

In 1994, 76 million tonnes of fish were caught in marine and island waters for direct human consumption (another 33 million tonnes were used for fishmeal and fish oil, and in other non-food uses). Fish currently comprise about 19 per cent of the less developed countries' animal protein intake, or 5 per cent of the total protein intake from both plant and animal protein.

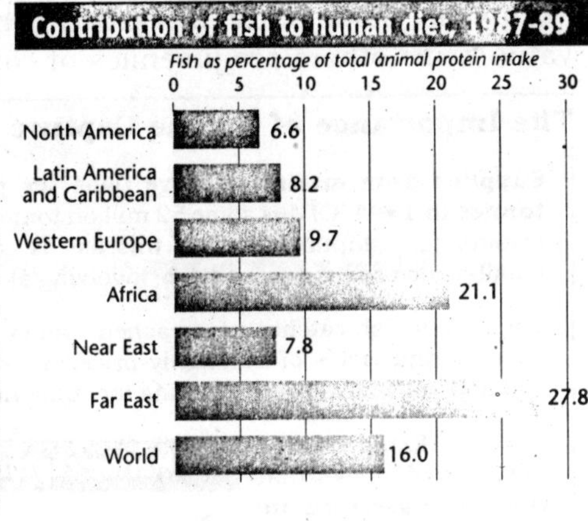

In many countries, fisheries are important to the food security of populations living in coastal areas, along river banks and on small islands. Fish play an even more important role in the nutrition of people living in the Low-income Food-Deficit Countries than they do elsewhere.

Fish Supply and Demand

Projections of demand for fish for food in the year 2010 are in the range of 110-120 million tonnes a year, a substantial increase from the 75-80 million tonnes that characterized the mid-1990s. Projections of supply for 2010 are less precise but the most optimistic projections fall within the range of the above demand. Fish prices appear set to increase and in some areas. For example, in sub-saharan Africa, South Asia and some Small Island Developing States, supplies per caput may fall.

About 80 per cent of the world's fish catch is currently produced from capture fisheries, the rest from aquaculture. But fishermen are having a difficult time competing for a limited resource where rates of capture have, in some areas, been driven down. This is leading to dispute and conflict, and threatens the resource base itself.

Disparities between supply and demand are worsened by wasteful methods of catching and processing fish. As much as 27 million tonnes of fish may be discarded each year. Some of the discarded fish have no commercial value while others are juveniles of commercial species.

The Importance of Marine Capture

Supplies from marine capture fisheries peaked at 85.2 million tonnes in 1994. Of this some 52 million tonnes was available for direct human consumption. Most of this fish is caught and processed by small-scale producers in a trade involving at least 100 million people.

The limit to fish catches was reached some years ago for most marine species, and yields of the highly-priced sea-bottom species (such as cod and sole) have been declining for some time.

FAO has found that 44 per cent of stocks that have been assessed are being exploited at their maximum or close to it; 25 per cent are depleted. Overfishing not only depletes resources, it also leads to conflict between states, regions and fishing groups. This is increasingly recognized by all concerned and remedial action has been initiated. Aggregate data on the fishing vessels of the world show that the globe fleet has started to decrease in size.

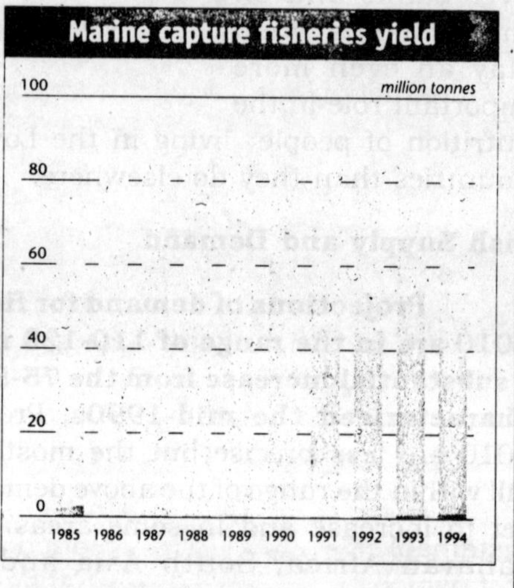

Expanding Through Aquaculture

Since fish is such a nutritious food, most solutions are aimed at increasing supply to meet demand, rather than reducing demand to meet supplies. Supplies can be increased from capture fisheries and aquaculture - but because more and more fisherman who exploit wild stocks are reaching the upper limits of what can be taken sustainably, the major prospects of increasing supplies lie in aquaculture or using aquaculture technology to support fisheries, as in sea reaching. Aquaculture is already growing rapidly, particularly in developing countries and in Asia (see Fact Sheet *Aquaculture Offers Cause for Hope*). It is possible that total production from aquaculture could rise from 19 million tonnes in 1994 to as much as 39 million tonnes by the year 2010.

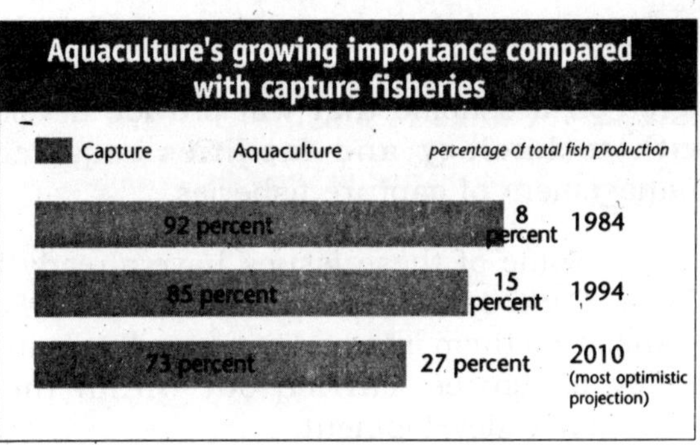

In the short term - the next two decades - very effort must also be made to sustain yields from capture fisheries, even though this inevitably gives rise to social and cultural problems, as well as technical and economic ones, resulting from too many fishermen chasing an inadequate resource.

Saving Marine Capture Fisheries

High on the International Agenda for achieving for sustainable fisheries will be a reduction in the world's fishing fleet, which currently stands at about 3.5 million vessels, a third of which are decked. Major savings will have to be made on high proportion of fish that are simply discarded at sea because they are the wrong size or have a lower commercial value than the species sought.

Ideas will have to change too. The old idea everyone can have free and open access to fish resources anywhere in the world will have to go. Instead fish resources must be carefully managed and their exploitation strictly controlled by legislation that is forward-looking rather than simply reactive.

The true value of fish will also have to be recognized and sustainable fishing assured. Developed countries (importers) and developing countries (exporters) need to agree on a scheme that will provide developing countries with technology and facilities required for effective management of capture fisheries.

Some of these issues have already been set out in FAO's *Code of Conduct for Responsible Fisheries* (1995). Translating them into real action will require a series of new policy measures, carried out within the framework of sustainable development.

The Kyoto Conference

The international Conference on the sustainable Contribution of Fisheries to Food Production (the Kyoto Conference) was held by the Government of Japan in collaboration with FAO in Kyoto during 4-9 December 1995. Attended by 95 states, the conference produced a declaration and plan of Action which

- Reiterate the need for better management of capture fishing and its environmental impact, essentially to stabilize capture fish supplies;
- Identify actions to promote a better use of existing fish supplies; and
- Identify actions aimed at providing a congenial economic and legal environment for aquaculture.

The key point of the Declaration is that projected shortfalls for 2010 can be reduced by

- Improving assessments and monitoring of fish stocks;
- Strengthening regional cooperation;
- Reducing excess fishing capacity;
- Improving information exchange;
- Reducing waste during fish capture;
- Strengthening research on environmentally-sound forms of aquaculture; and
- Improving technical and financial assistance to developing countries.

14

FORESTS AND FOOD SECURITY

Forests play a crucial role in providing security. They are veritable storehouses of biological diversity, and forest products are the mainstay of households worldwide. As living systems, forests have a vital role in maintaining the ecological base for food security. Even so, it is common to find that public and private planners "fail to see the forest for trees", understanding or even ignoring the value of these resources.

Forests for Food

Forests contribute directly to the diets of forest dwellers and of many who live far beyond the woods. Forest fruits, nuts and berries, for instance, are popular with urban as well as rural consumers. These and many other forest foods. add variety and flavour to diets while providing essential vitamins, minerals, fats and proteins. During times of seasonal food shortages or emergencies - caused, for example, by droughts, floods or wars - forest foods also offer vital insurance against malnutrition or famine. Leaves - used as flavoring in soups, stews and relishes - and mushrooms are the most common forest foods. Animal foods include a large variety of both invertebrates, such as edible insects, and vertebrates, including mammles, birds and fish.

Forests for Income

For rural people, especially those with little or no

land of their own, forests may provide the main source of cash income. This income does not come from wood harvesting only. Non-wood forest resources can often generate greater, more sustainable incomes than can be gained from the same land when used for agriculture or logging. World trade in rattan, for instance, is worth US$2000 million annually. **In India alone, forest-based industries support 30 million people.**

Forests for Livestock

Forests provide fodder and rangeland for 30 to 40 million pastoralists worldwide who herd some 4 000 million cattle, goats and sheep. Trees help to protect pastoral rangelands, providing shade for cattle and crops and thereby supporting livestock production. Nonetheless, while livestock are increasing in number, the area available for grazing is being reduced because of conversion to crop production.

Forests and the Environment

Forests and trees greatly contribute to maintaining the ecological balance. The integration of trees within agricultural schemes sustains crop production by improving soil fertility. **Trees help to control water and wind erosion and they recycle vital nutrients, such as nitrogen, back into the soil. Trees also grow where agricultural crops might fail, allowing production on marginal lands.** As they grow, trees absorb and store carbon dioxide (CO_2). Deforestation - especially by burning - releases a great amount of stored CO_2 into the atmosphere, contributing to global warming.

Forests and Medicine

For 75 to 90 per cent of the people in developing countries, natural products represent the only source of medicine. **The active ingredients found in 25 per cent of prescription drugs come from medicinal plants.** Nearly all of the so-called alternative medicines are also based on plant extracts. The estimated value of plant-based drugs nearly US$45 000 million a year.

Cases in Point

- In the Peruvian Amazon, more than 80 per cent of animal protein comes from **bushmeat**. In Botswana, the springhare provides meat equivalent to that from some 20 000 heads of cattle.
- In the United States, non-wood forest products are worth more than $130 million a year in industry revenues and employ at least 10 000 people full time. The bank of the Western Yew trees is harvested in quantities exceeding 350 tonnes a year. It yields the drug taxol, an anti-cancer agent. Formerly a throwaway by-product in the eyes of local foresters, trade in **yew bark** now provides an alternative livelihood for an army of local "pickers", including many loggers who were out of work as a result of declining markets in timber and wood products.
- **Rattan** is the most important non-timber forest product of southeast Asia, contributing to a world trade of about US$2 000 million a year. In Indonesia, the rattan industry employs 83 000 to 100 000 people and exports are worth $90 million a year. In Malaysia, the annual turnover is $35 million, about half of which is exported.
- The per caput consumption of **mushrooms** during the rainy season in Zimbabwe can be as high as 1.8 kg. The fungi, commonly valued as meat substitutes, supply surprisingly large amounts of protein (up to 45 g per 100 g dry weight in some cases) and essential minerals. Over 20 tonnes of mushrooms are gathered and consumed by the 700 000 residents of the Upper Shaba area of Zaire every year.

Forests and Biological Diversity

Forests are among the most important living genebanks on earth. Many of the foods we consume today originated as wild crops in the forests. Genetic improvement has much to gain from existing wild species, which may posses valuable traits that can be incorporated into their cultivated relatives to make them hardier and more disease resistant. **If deforestation is not controlled, however, it could be the single greatest cause of species loss over the next 50 years.**

Forests for Energy

Wood energy is drawing increasing attention as an environmentally friendly source of energy. Wood is still people's main source of fuel for cooking, processing and preserving food, and will continue to be for many years to come. **Worldwide, 2 000 million people depend on wood for cooking, a basic step in ensuring proper nutrition. In many developing countries, fuelwood supplies as much as 97 per cent of total energy consumption.** Wood-based energy system are the most readily available in many areas and, when properly managed, they are not only versatile and sustainable but also effective in generating income and jobs.

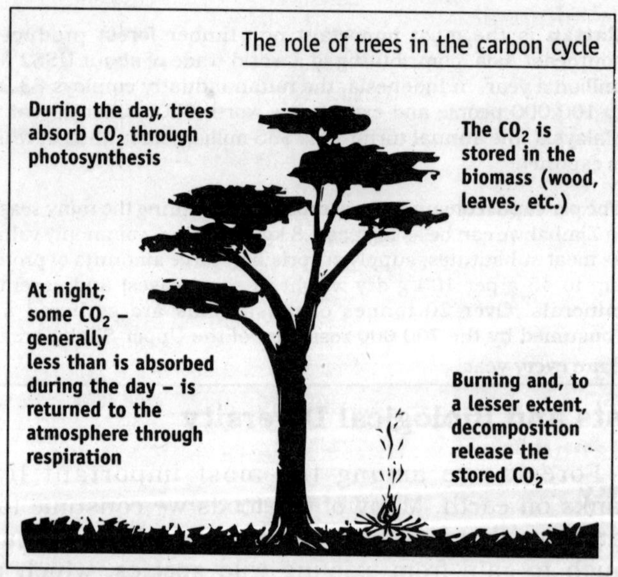

Forests for Habitat

Forests are home to 300 million people around the world who depend on shifting cultivation, hunting and gathering to survive. The needs of forest dwellers have often been overlooked in development plans and their lives are becoming increasingly precarious as population pressures encroach on the land available for shifting cultivation.

Forests and Culture

Traditionally, the importance of forests and trees has been recognized by cultures worldwide. Trees have featured throughout history in religion and folklore and are often described as God's gift to humans. They are recognized for their regenerative nature and are associated with health, marital harmony and longevity. For the use and other reasons, forests are carefully protected by traditional societies.

Forests and Food Security

The effective integration of forests and agricultural, economic and development schemes - carefully planned according to local needs and circumstances - has

What forests provide

Food
- leaves
- seeds and nuts
- roots and tubers
- "bushmeat"
- insects
- honey
- mushrooms
- fruits
- saps and gums
- oils and fats

Fibre
- silk
- rattan
- jute
- bamboo

Fertilizers
- compost
- nitrogen and other nutrients

Fodder
- leaves
- shrubs
- grasses

Fuel
- wood
- charcoal

Medicines
- prescription drugs
- traditional plant remedies
- teas and herbs

Essences
- perfumes
- cosmetics
- herbs
- gums
- saps
- resins
- syrups

Biological diversity
- food crops and wild relatives
- grasses
- ornamental plants
- animals

Environment
- shade
- windbreaks
- erosion control
- filters of toxins
- breeding grounds

Recreation
- parks
- wildlife reserves

Timber products

great potential for increasing food security for present and future generations. On the other hand, the continuing loss of vital forest resources cause damage that is, in many cases, irreversible. By designing and implementing integrated schemes for the management of forests at the national and international levels, governments can strengthen and renew their crucial role in relieving the burden of hunger and poverty throughout the world.

15

ENVIRONMENT AND FOOD SECURITY

Feeding another 3 billion people by the year 2030 will require rapid gains in agricultural production. Achieving those gains without damaging natural resources on which both agriculture and life itself depend will require a modified approach to food production compared with the past - an approach that builds on ecological principles such as diversity, resilience and efficient energy use.

Limited Resources, Vulnerable Resources

In order to meet minimum requirements of a growing population, food production will need to double over the next 30 years. Yet the natural resources required to produce this additional food - such as soil, water and the diversity of crops and livestock - are finite and vulnerable to degradation.

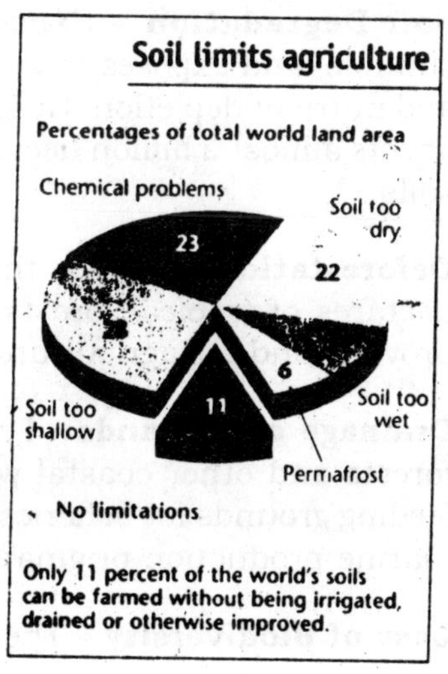

Only 11 percent of the world's soils can be farmed without being irrigated, drained or otherwise improved.

Between 1950 and 1995, for example, rapid population growth

cut in half the amount of cultivated land per person - from more than half a hectare to barely a quarter. Because only about 11 per cent of the world's land is really suited to agriculture, the amount of arable land per person will continue shrinking. By the year 2020, for example, Southeast Asia will have only 0.09 hectares per person - an area barely one-tenth the size of a soccer field.

Per caput water availability is also falling rapidly. In Africa, for example, the amount of water available per person has dropped almost 75 per cent since 1950 - from over 20,000 cubic metres a year to a little 5,000 cubic metres. Experts define countries where the amount of water available for all purposes, including agriculture and industry, amounts to less than 1,000 cubic metres per person per year. **More than 230 million people - mostly in Africa and the Near East - now live in such countries.**

The Price of Expanded Production

Pushing Against Resource Limits to increase food production can damage or degrade natural resources in many ways:

Soil Degradation - Expansion of agriculture onto less suitable land exposes fragile soils to the dangers of erosion and nutrient depletion. Human-induced degradation already affects almost 2 billion hectares, or 15 per cent of the world's soils.

Deforestation - During the 1980s, more than 15 million hectares of tropical forests were lost each year, mainly to provide land for agriculture.

Drainage of Wetlands - Felling and drainage of mangrove forests and other coastal wetlands destroys spawning and feeding grounds for fisheries. About 95 per cent of the world's marine production originates from coastal ecosystems.

Loss of Biodiversity - The conversion of forests and other natural habitats to food production has been the primary reason for the rapid loss the biological diversity that threatens between 5 and 20 per cent of some groups of vertebrates and plants with extinction.

Overfishing - almost 70 per cent of those stocks of marine fisheries for which assessments are available are being fished at levels close to or beyond the maximum sustainable yield.

Livestock for Sustainable Agriculture

Mixed farming systems that include livestock have many advantages over 'crops-only' agriculture. Mixed systems produce a bigger range of products, reduce risks and can be more productive than systems that rely exclusively on either crops or animals.

Intensive Production - Promise and Peril

Applying intensive production techniques to increase output from lands already under cultivation could both provide enough food to meet the needs of an expanding population and relieve pressure on marginal lands and vulnerable ecosystems. Research stations typically obtain yields more than double those achieved by farmers under similar conditions.

But intensive food production can also take a heavy toll on the environment.

Poorly Managed Irrigation can lead to salinization and waterlogging. Some 30 million hectares of irrigated land have been severely damaged by poor drainage and accumulation of salt in the soil.

Reliance on a Few High-Yielding Varieties of plants and livestock has eroded biodiversity within the limited number of species used for agriculture, increasing vulnerability to pests and diseases. Thirty per cent of all breeds of livestock have less than 20 breeding males or less than 1000 breeding females remaining.

Intensive Aquaculture Systems, such as cage culture of salmon and large-scale shrimp culture in coastal areas, can cause excessive nutrient enrichment of water bodies, degradation of wetlands and the loss of biological diversity from the introduction of exotic species.

One key advantage of mixed systems is that livestock can be fed on crops residues and other products that would otherwise pose a major waste disposal problem. For example, livestock can be fed straw, damaged fruit and grains, household wastes, catering wastes in urban areas, canning and juicing residues, and fish processing wastes.

Integration of livestock and crops allows nutrients to be recycled more efficiently on the farm Manure is itself a valuable fertilizer, containing 8 kg of phosphorus and 16 kg

Does Livestock Development Harm the Environment?

Livestock development is often questioned on environmental grounds. Common criticisms include:

- **Demand for Pasture Causes Deforestation** - this has occurred in South America but it results from vested interest rather than livestock production itself.
- **Overgazing in Semi-arid Areas Destroys Vegetation and Leads to Desertification** - also true, at least in Africa where millions of pastoralists depend for their survival on livestock; damage could be lessened by providing better support for sustainable pastoralism in areas where crop production would be impossible or very risky. Note : due to soil and climate many areas are only suitable for grazing. In fact, permanent pasture is the most widespread land use, occupying 3.4 billion hectares.
- **Overstocking of Pastures Leads to Soil Erosion** - not necessarily, since livestock can be grazed on fodder trees and hedgerows, or stall-fed, in which case they provide valuable manure for soil enrichment and conditioning.
- **Ruminant Production Leads to the Production of the Greenhouse Gas Methane** - true, but the amounts are small and can be reduced by balanced diets.
- **Livestock Consume Cereals that would be Better Fed Directly to Humans** - not necessarily; most of the cereals fed to livestock are in developed countries, and the rural poor in developing countries could not afford to buy such 'surplus' cereals anyway; furthermore, livestock can be fed alternatives such as urea-treated straw, molasses, chopped sugarcane; **in fact, livestock can be an important means of converting other unusable vegetation and crop by-products into high value milk and meat.**

of potassium to the tonne. Adding manure to the soil not only fertilizes it but also improves its structure and water retention.

Where livestock are used to graze the vegetation under plantations of coconut, oil-palm and rubber, as in Malaysia, the cost of weed control can be dramatically reduced, sometimes by as much as 40 per cent. In Colombia sheep are sometimes used to control weeds in sugarcane.

livestock for draught power
livestock for food
livestock for weed control
livestock for manure
sustainable agriculture
livestock for waste disposal
livestock for fuel and biogas
livestock for extra income
livestock to reduce risk

Draught animal power is widely used for cultivation, transport, water lifting and powering food processing equipment. Using draught animal power reduces the need for foreign exchange to buy expensive tractors and fuel. It is estimated that 52 per cent of the cultivated area in the developing countries excluding China, is farmed exclusively with draught animals. Animal traction increases the area under cultivation, bringing heavy but potentially very productive soils into production.

Finally, cow dung is a highly valued fuel used for cooking and heating in many countries. While dung that is burnt is lost as a fertilizer, its use for fuel reduces the demand for wood and fossil fuel, and the dung ash can itself be used as a fertilizer. Alternatively manure can be used to generate methane or biogas - about 25 kg of fresh cow dung makes one cubic metre of biogas which can be used to provide energy for,light, heat or motive power.

Boosting Livestock Production

Livestock is a neglected sub-sector; funding for livestock project has declined dramatically since 1974. One reason is that intensive livestock production in developed countries is seen as 'grain-hungry' and polluting. However livestock production in developing countries need not result in either effect; in fact, some livestock projects have been highly successful - witness the beef Fattening project in China that used cereal straw treated with urea to feed beef cattle and Operation Flood that helped establish a modern dairy industry in India.

If the world's livestock potential is to be properly realized, it is important that:

- public policy facilitate fair commodity prices and favour better use of local resources;
- people participate in the formation of policies for the management of common land and rangeland;
- care be taken to use alternative feeds that do not compete with human food;
- increased funds and other resources be devoted to livestock development, particularly for small farmers.

16

ROME DECLARATION ON WORLD FOOD SECURITY

We, the Heads of State and Government[1], or our representatives, gathered at the World Food Summit at the invitation of the Food and Agriculture Organization of the United Nations, reaffirm the right of everyone to have access to safe and nutritious food, consistent with the right to adequate food and the fundamental right of everyone to be free from hunger.

We pledge our political will and our common and national commitment to achieving food security for all and to an ongoing effort to eradicate hunger in all countries, with an immediate view to reducing the number of undernourished people to half their present level no later than 2015.

We consider it intolerable that more than 800 million people throughout the world, and particularly in developing countries, do not have enough food to meet their basic nutritional needs. This situation is unacceptable. Food supplies have increased substantially, but constraints on access to food and continuing inadequacy of household and national incomes to purchase food, instability of supply and demand, as well as natural and man-made disasters, prevent basic food needs from being fulfilled. The problems of hunger and food insecurity have global dimensions and are likely to persist, and even increase dramatically in some regions,

[1] When "Government" is used, it means as well the European Community within the areas of competence.

unless urgent, determined and concerted action is taken, given the anticipated increase in the world's population and the stress on natural resources.

We reaffirm that a peaceful, stable and enabling political, social and economic environment is the essential foundation which will enable States to give adequate priority to food security and poverty eradication. Democracy, promotion and protection of all human rights and fundamental freedoms, including the right to development, and the full and equal participation of men and women are essential for achieving sustainable food security for all.

Poverty is a major cause of food insecurity and sustainable progress in poverty eradication is critical to improve access to food. Conflict, terrorism, corruption and environmental degradation also contribute significantly to food insecurity. Increased food production, including staple food, must be undertaken. This should happen within the framework of sustainable management of natural resources, elimination of unsustainable patterns of consumption and production, particularly in industrialized countries, and early stabilization of the world population. We acknowledge the fundamental contribution to food security by women, particularly in rural areas of developing countries, and the need to ensure equality between men and women. Revitalization of rural areas must also be a priority to enhance social stability and help redress the excessive rate of rural-urban migration confronting many countries.

We emphasize the urgency of taking action now to fulfil our responsibility to achieve food security for present and future generations. Attaining food security is a complex task for which the primary responsibility rests with individual governments. They have to develop an enabling environment and have policies that ensure peace, as well as social, political and economic stability and equity and gender equality. We express our deep concern over the persistence of hunger which, on such a scale, constitutes a threat both to national societies and, through a variety of ways, to the stability of the international community itself. Within the global framework, governments should also cooperate actively with one another and with United Nations organizations, financial institutions, intergovernmental and non-governmental organizations, and public and private sectors, on programmes directed toward the achievement of food security for all.

Food should not be used as an instrument for political and economic pressure. We reaffirm the importance of international cooperation and solidarity as well as the necessity of refraining from unilateral measures not in accordance with the international law and the Charter of the United Nations and that endanger food security.

We recognize the need to adopt policies conducive to investment in human resource development, research and infrastructure for achieving food security. We must encourage generation of employment and incomes, and promote equitable access to productive and financial resources. We agree that trade is a key element in achieving food security. We agree to pursue food trade and overall trade policies that will encourage our producers and consumers to utilize available resources in an economically sound and sustainable manner. We recognize the importance for food security for sustainable agriculture, fisheries, forestry and rural development in low as well as high potential areas. We acknowledge the fundamental role of farmers, fishers, foresters, indigenous people and their communities, and all other people involved in food sector, and of their organizations, supported by effective research and extension, in attaining food security. Our sustainable development policies will promote full participation and empowerment of people, especially women, an equitable distribution of income, access to health care and education, and opportunities for youth. Particular attention should be given to those who cannot produce or procure enough food for an adequate diet, including those affected by war, civil strife, natural disaster or climate related ecological changes. We are conscious of the need for urgent action to combat pests, drought, and natural resource degradation including desertification, overfishing and erosion of biological diversity.

We are determined to make efforts to mobilize, and optimize the allocation and utilization of, technical and financial resources from all sources, including external debt relief for developing countries, to reinforce national actions implement sustainable food security policies.

Convinced that the multifaceted character of food security necessitates concerted national action, and effective international efforts to supplement and reinforce national action, we make following commitments:

- we will ensure an enabling political, social, and economic environment designed to create the best conditions for the eradication of poverty and durable peace, based on full and equal participation of women and men, which is most conducive to achieving sustainable food security for all;
- we will implement policies aimed at eradicating poverty and inequality and improving physical and economic access by all, at all times, to sufficient, nutritionally adequate and safe food and its effective utilization;
- we will pursue participatory and sustainable food, agriculture, fisheries, forestry and rural development policies and practices in high and low potential areas, which are essential to adequate and reliable food supplies at the household, national, regional and global levels, and combat pests, drought and desertification, considering the multifunctional character of agriculture;
- we will strive to ensure that food, agricultural trade and overall trade policies are conducive of fostering food security for all through a fair and market-oriented world trade system;
- we will endeavour to prevent and be prepared for natural disasters and man-made emergencies and to meet transitory and emergency food requirements in ways that encourage recovery, rehabilitation, development and a capacity to satisfy future needs;

- we will promote allocation and use of public and private investments to foster human resources, sustainable food, agriculture, fisheries and forestry systems, and rural development, in high and low potential areas;
- we will implement, monitor, and follow-up this Plan of Action at all levels in cooperation with the international community.

We pledge our actions and support to implement the World Food Summit Plan of Action.

Rome, 13 November 1996

17

WORLD FOOD SUMMIT PLAN OF ACTION

1. The Rome Declaration on World Food Security and the World Food Summit Plan of Action lay the foundations for diverse paths to a common objective - food security, at the individual, household, national, regional and global levels. Food security exists when all people, at all times, have physical and economic access to sufficient, safe and nutritious food to meet their dietary needs and food preferences for an active and healthy life. In this regard, concerted action at all levels is required. Each nation must adopt a strategy consistent with its resources and capacities to achieve its individual goals and, at the same time, cooperate regionally and internationally in order to organize collective solutions to global issues of food security. In a world of increasingly interlinked institutions, societies and economies, coordinated efforts and shared responsibilities are essential.

2. Poverty eradication is essential to improve access to food. The vast majority of those who are undernourished, either cannot produce or cannot afford to buy enough food. They have inadequate access to means of production such as land, water, inputs, improved seeds and plants, appropriate technologies and farm credit. In addition, wars, civil strife, natural disasters, climate related ecological changes and environment degradation have adversely affected millions of people. Although food assistance may be provided to ease their plight, it is not

a long term solution to the underlying causes of food insecurity. It is important to maintain an adequate capacity in the international community to provide food aid, whenever it is required, in response to emergencies. Equitable access to stable food supplies should be ensured.

3. A peaceful and stable environment in every country is a fundamental condition for the attainment of sustainable food security. Governments are responsible for creating an enabling environment for private and group initiatives to devote their skills, efforts and resources, and in particular investment, towards the common goal of food for all. This should be undertaken with the cooperation and participation of all members of society. Farmers, fishers and foresters and other food producers and providers, have critical roles in achieving food security, and their full involvement and enablement are crucial for success.

4. Poverty, hunger and malnutrition are some of the causes of accelerated migration from rural to urban areas in developing countries. The largest population shift of all times is now under way. Unless these problems are addressed in an appropriate and timely fashion, the political, economic and social stability of many countries and regions may well be seriously affected, perhaps even compromising world peace. It is necessary to target those people and areas suffering most from hunger and malnutrition and identify causes and take remedial action to improve the situation. A more complete, user-friendly source of information at all levels would enable this.

5. Availability of enough food for all can be attained. The 5.8 billion people in the world today have, on average, 15 per cent more food per person than the global population of 4 billion people had 20 years ago. Yet, further large increases in world food production, through the sustainable management of natural resources, are

required to feed a growing population, and achieving improved diets. Increased production, including traditional crops and their products, in efficient combination with food imports, reserves, and international trade can strengthen food security and address regional disparities. Food aid is one of the many instruments which can help to promote food security. Long term investment in research and in cataloguing and conserving genetic resources, particularly at the national level, is essential. The link between sufficient food supplies and household food security must be ensured.

6. Harmful seasonal and inter-annual instability of food supplies can be reduced. Progress should include targeting on minimizing the vulnerability to, and impact of, climate fluctuation and pests and disease. To effect timely transfers of supplies to deficit areas and the conservation and sustainable use of biodiversity, use should be made, in efficient combination, of climate early warning systems, transfer and utilization of appropriate agriculture,[1] fishery and forestry technologies, production, and reliable trade, storage and financial mechanisms. Natural and man-made disasters can often be anticipated or even prevented, and response must be timely effective and assist recovery.

7. Unless national governments and the international community address the multifaceted causes underlying food security, the number of hungry and malnourished people will remain very high in developing countries, particularly in Africa south of the Sahara; and sustainable food security will not be achieved. This situation is unacceptable. This Plan of Action envisages an ongoing effort to eradicate hunger in all countries, with an immediate view to reducing the number of undernourished people to half their present level no later than 2015, and a mid-term review to ascertain whether it is possible to achieve this target by 2010.

---

[1] In this document "agriculture" and "agricultural" include livestock.

8. The resources required for investment will be generated mostly from domestic, private and public sources. The international community has a key role to play in supporting the adoption of appropriate national policies and, where necessary and appropriate, in providing technical and financial assistance to assist developing countries and countries with economies in transition in fostering food security.

9. The multi-dimensional nature of the follow-up to the World Food Summit includes at the national, intergovernmental and inter-agency levels. The international community, and the UN system, including FAO, as well as other agencies and bodies according to their mandates, have important contributions to the implementations of the World Food Summit Plan of Action. The FAO Committee on World Food Security (CFS) will have responsibility to monitor the implementation of the Plan of Action.

10. Reaching sustainable world food security is part and parcel of achieving the social, economic, environmental and human development objectives agreed upon in recent international conferences. The world Food Summit Plan of Action builds on consensus reached in these fora and is based on the conviction that although the world is faced with major food insecurity, solutions to these problems exist. If all parties at local, national, regional and international levels make determined and sustained efforts, then the overall goal of food for all, at all times, will be achieved.

11. The Plan of Action of the World Food Summit is in conformity with the purposes and principles of the UN Charter and international law and strives to consolidate the results of other UN conferences since 1990 on subjects having a bearing on food security.

12. The implementation of the recommendations contained in this Plan of Action is the Sovereign right and responsibility of each State through national laws and the formulation of strategies, policies, programmes, and

development priorities, in conformity with all human rights and fundamental freedoms, including the right to development, and the significance of and the full respect for various religious and ethical values, cultural backgrounds and philosophical convictions of individuals and their communities should contribute to the full enjoyment by all of their human rights in order to achieve the objective of food security for all.

COMMITMENT ONE

We will ensure an enabling political, social, and economic environment designed to create the best conditions for the eradication of poverty and for durable peace, based on full and equal participation of women and men, which is most conducive to achieving sustainable food security for all.

The Basis for Action

13. A growing world population and the urgency of eradicating hunger and malnutrition call for determined policies and effective actions. A peaceful, stable and enabling political, social and economic environment is the essential foundation which will enable States to give adequate priority to food security, poverty eradication and sustainable agriculture, fisheries, forestry and rural development. Promotion and protection of all human rights and fundamental freedoms, including the right to development and the progressive realization of the right to adequate food for all and the full and equal participation of men and women are also indispensable to our goal of achieving sustainable food security for all.

Objectives and Actions

14. **Objective 1.1 :** To prevent and resolve conflicts peacefully and create a stable political environment, through respect for all human rights and fundamental freedoms, democracy, a transparent and effective legal framework,

transparent and accountable governance and administration in all public and private, national and international institutions, and effective and equal participation of all people, at all levels, in decisions and actions that affect their food security.

To this end, governments, in partnership, as appropriate, with all actors of civil society, will where not already accomplished:

(a) In cooperation, as appropriate, with the international community, assure and reinforce peace, by developing conflict prevention mechanisms, settling disputes by peaceful means, as well as by promoting tolerance, non-violence and respect for diversity;

(b) Develop policy making, legislative and implementation processes that are democratic, transparent, participatory, empowering, responsive to changing circumstances and most conducive to achieving sustainable food security for all;

(c) Promote and strengthen well-functioning legal and judicial systems to protect the rights of all people;

(d) Recognize and support indigenous people and their communities in their pursuit of economic and social development, with full respect for their identity, traditions, forms of social organization and cultural values.

Furthermore, governments, in partnership with all actors of civil society and with support of international institutions, will, as appropriate:

(e) Strengthen rules and mechanisms existing in international and regional organizations to seek, in accordance with the UN Charter, the prevention and solution of conflicts which cause or exacerbate food insecurity as well as to settle disputes by peaceful means, promote tolerance, non-violence, respect for diversity and observance of international law.

15. **Objective 1.2** : To ensure stable economic conditions and implement development strategies which encourage the full potential of private and public, individual and collective initiatives for sustainable, equitable, economic and social development which also integrate population and environmental concerns.

To this end, governments, and as appropriate, in partnership with all actors of civil society, will:

(a) Promote policies in order to foster a national and international environment that is more conducive to sustainable, equitable economic and social development;

(b) Establish legal and other mechanisms, as appropriate, that advance land reform, recognize and protect property, water, and use rights, to enhance access for the poor and women to resources. Such mechanisms should also promote conservation and sustainable use of natural resources (such as land, water and forests), lower risks, and encourage investment;

(c) Fully integrate population concern into development strategies, plans, and decision-making, including factors affecting migration, and devise appropriate population policies, programmes and family planning services, consistent with the Report and the Programme of Action of the International Conference on Population and Development, Cairo 1994.

16. **Objective 1.3** : To ensure gender equality and empowerment of women.

To this end, government will:

(a) Support and implement commitments made at the Fourth

World Conference on women, Beijing 1995, that a gender perspective is mainstreamed in all policies;

(b) Promote women's full and equal participation in the economy, and for this purpose introduce and enforce gender-sensitive legislation providing women with source and equal access to and control over productive resources including credit, land and water;

(c) Ensure that institutions provide equal access for women;

(d) Provide equal gender opportunities for education and training in food production, processing and marketing;

(e) Tailor extension and technical services to women producers and increase the number of women advisors and agents;

(f) Improve the collection, dissemination and use of gender-disaggregated data in agriculture, fisheries, forestry and rural development;

(g) Focus research efforts on the division of labour and on income access and control within the household;

(h) Gather information on women's traditional knowledge and skills in agriculture, fisheries, forestry and natural resources management.

17 **Objective 1.4** : To encourage national solidarity and provide equal opportunities for all, at all levels, in social, economic and political life, particularly in respect of vulnerable and disadvantaged groups and persons.

To this end, governments, in partnership with all actors of civil society, will, as appropriate:

(a) Support investment in human resource development such as health, education, literacy and other skills training, which are essential to sustainable development, including agriculture, fisheries, forestry and rural development;

(b) Enact or strengthen policies to combat discrimination against members of socially vulnerable and disadvantaged groups, and persons belonging to minorities, with particular attention to their rights to land and other property, and to their access to credit, education and training, commercial markets and food security programmes;

(c) Enact legislation and establish institutional structures that provide opportunities for youth and enhance the special contribution that women can make to ensuring family and child nutrition with due emphasis on the importance of breast-feeding for infants;

(d) Give special attention to promoting and protecting the interests and needs of the child, particularly the girl child, in food security programmes, consisting with the World Summit for Children - Convention on the Rights of the Child, New York 1990.

COMMITMENT TWO

We will implement policies aimed at eradicating poverty and inequality and improving physical and economic access by all, at all times, to sufficient, nutritionally adequate and safe food and its effective utilization.

The Basis for Action

18. Assured access to nutritionally adequate and safe food is essential for individual welfare and for national, social and economic development, in accordance with the World Declaration on Nutrition, International Conference on Nutrition (ICN), Rome 1992. Every country in the world has vulnerable and disadvantaged individuals, households and groups who cannot meet their own needs. Seventy percent of all poor are women, which should be taken into consideration when preparing poverty eradicating action. Even where and when overall food supplies are adequate, poverty impedes access by all to

the quantity and variety of foods needed to meet the population's needs. Rapid population growth and rural poverty have resulted excessive migration to urban areas with serious negative social, economic, environmental and nutritional impact. Unless extraordinary efforts are undertaken, an unacceptably large portion of the world's population, particularly in developing countries, could still be chronically undernourished by the year 2010 with additional suffering due to acute periodic shortages of food. Contributing to malnutrition is the lack of adequate food utilization which, in this context, is the proper digestion and absorption of nutrients in food by the human body and requires adequate diet, water salinization, health services, and health education.

Objectives and Actions

19 **Objective 2.1**: To pursue poverty eradication, among both urban and rural poor, and sustainable food security for all as a policy priority and to promote, through sound national policies. Secure and gainful employment and equitable and equal access to productive resources such as land, water and credit, so as to maximize the incomes of the poor.

To this end, governments, in partnership with all actors of civil society, as appropriate, will:

(a) Review and adopt policies to pursue the eradication of hunger and attain sustainable food security at all household and national levels as a top policy priority, and make every effort to eliminate obstacles such as unemployment and lack of access to factors of production that adversely affect the attainment of food security, and implement the relevant commitments they entered into at the World Summit for Social Development, Copenhagen 1995;

(b) Develop human skills and capacities through basic

education and pre- and on-the-job training;

(c) Adopt policies that create conditions which encourage stable employment, especially in rural areas, including off-farm jobs, so as to provide sufficient earnings to facilitate the purchase of basic necessities as well as encourage labour intensive technologies where appropriate:

(d) Pursue sound economic, agriculture, fisheries, forestry and land reform policies that will permit farmers, fishers, foresters and other food producers, particularly women, to earn a fair return from their labour, capital and management, and encourage conservation and sustainable management of natural resources including in marginal areas;

(e) Improve equal access, by men and women, to land and other natural and productive resources, in particular, where necessary, through the effective implementation of land reform and the promotion of efficient utilization of natural and agricultural resources and resettlement on new lands, where feasible;

(f) Promote access, by farmers and farming communities, to genetic resources for food and agriculture.

20. **Objective 2.2** : To enable food insecure households, families and individuals to meet their food and nutritional requirements and to seek to assist those who are unable to do so.

To this end, governments, in partnership with all actors of civil society, as appropriate, will:

(a) Develop and periodically update, where necessary, a national food insecurity and vulnerability information and mapping system, indicating areas and populations, including at local level, affected by or at-risk of hunger and malnutrition, and elements contributing to food insecurity, making maximum use of existing data and other information systems in order to avoid duplication of efforts;

(b) Implement, where appropriate, cost-effective public works programmes for the unemployed and underemployed in regions of food insecurity;

(c) Develop within available resources well targeted social welfare and nutrition safety nets to meet the needs of the food insecure, particularly needy people, children, and the infirm.

21 **Objective 2.3** : To ensure that food supplies are safe, physically and economically accessible, appropriate and adequate to meet the energy and nutrient needs of the population.

To this end, governments, in partnership with all actors of civil society, as appropriate, will:

(a) Monitor the availability and nutritional adequacy of food supplies and reserve stocks, giving particular attention to areas to high risk of food insecurity, to nutritionally vulnerable groups, and to areas where seasonal variations have important nutritional implications;

(b) Apply measures, in conformity with the Agreement on the Application of Sanitary and Phytosanitary Measures and other relevant international agreements, that ensure the quality and safety of food supply, particularly by strengthening normative and control activities in the areas of human, animal and plant health and safety;

(c) Encourage, where appropriate, the production and use of culturally appropriate, traditional and underutlilized food crops, including grains, oilseeds, pulses, root crops, fruits and vegetables, promoting home and, where appropriate, school gardens and urban agriculture, using sustainable technologies, and encourage the sustainable utilization of unused or underutilized fish resources;

(d) Develop and promote improved food processing, preservation and storage technologies to reduce post-harvest food losses, especially at the local level;

(e) Encourage rural households and communities to adopt low-coast technologies and innovative practices;

(f) Promote and support community-based food security and nutrition programmes that encourage self-reliance, utilizing participatory planning and implementing processes;

(g) Implement the goals of preventing and controlling specific micro-nutrient deficiencies as agreed a the ICN.

22. **Objective 2.4** : To promote access for all, especially the poor and members of vulnerable and disadvantaged groups, to basic education and primary health care provision in order to strengthen their capacity for self-reliance.

To this end, governments, in partnership with all actors of civil society, will:

(a) Promote access for all people, especially the poor and members of vulnerable and disadvantaged groups to primary health care, including reproductive health services consistent with the Report and the Programme of Action of the International Conference on Population and Development, Cairo 1994;

(b) Promote access to clean water and sanitation for all people, especially in poor communities and rural areas;

(c) Promote access to, and support for complete primary education, including, where appropriate, school feeding programmes, with particular attention to children in rural areas and to girls;

(d) Provide nutrition, sanitation, and health education for the public and promote technologies and training programmes on nutrition, home economics, environmental protection, food supply and health.

COMMITMENT THREE

We will pursue participatory and sustainable food, agriculture fisheries, forestry and rural development policies and practices in high and low potential areas, which are essential to adequate and reliable food supplies at the household, national, regional and global levels, and combat pests, drought and desertification, considering the multifunctional character of agriculture.

The Basis for Action

23. It is imperative that food production be increased, particularly in low-income, food-deficit countries, to meet the needs of the undernourished and food insecure, the additional food requirements resulting from population growth, demand for new food products due to rising standards of living and changes in consumption patterns. Production increases need to be achieved without further overburdening women farmers, while ensuring both productive capacity, sustainable management of natural resources and protection of the environment.

24. In many parts of the world, unsustainable and otherwise inadequate policies and programmes, inappropriate technologies, insufficient rural infrastructures and institutions, as well as pests and diseases, lead to inefficiency and wastage of natural and human resources, inputs and products. The resources base for food, agriculture, fisheries and forestry is under stress and is threatened by problems such as desertification, deforestation, overfishing, overcapacity and discards in fisheries, losses of biodiversity, as well as inefficient use of water, climate change and depletion of the ozone layer. This has a negative impact on both food security and the environment. The framework for sustainable agriculture, fisheries, forestry and rural development in relation to food security was elaborated in the Programme of Action

for Sustainable Development (Agenda 21) of the United Nations Conference on Environment and Development (UNCED), Rio de Janerio 1992, and recently expanded in both the Kyoto Declaration and Plan of Action on the Sustainable Contribution of Fisheries to Food Security (Kyoto Declaration and Plan of Action), 1995, and the Leipzig Declaration on and the Global Plan of Action for the Conservation and Sustainable Utilization of Plant Genetic Resources for Food and Agriculture (Leipzig Declaration and Global Plan of Action), 1996.

25. Expanding production in low-income food-deficit countries (LIFDCs) is frequently one of the primary means to increase the availability of food and income for those living in poverty. Most of the increases in food output of these countries, and of more developed regions, are expected to come from areas which have the agro-climatic potential to generate sufficient surpluses in economically and environmentally sound conditions, in particular to feed growing numbers of urban consumers. The generation of employment and income will raise effective demand in these areas, thereby stimulating production, economic diversification and rural development. In marginal areas and coastal communities with lower potential and fragile environments, there is also a need to increase food production through the provision of inputs and appropriate technology to reduce rural migration, but this should be based on sustainable management of resources and environment. Efficient land use for sustainable agricultural activity in many areas will also contribute significantly towards reducing the pressure to convert forests to agricultural land.

26. Food security depends, *inter alia,* on sustainable management of fish, forests, and wild life. In many indigenous communities, these resources are the principal sources of protein in the diet. The traditional knowledge within indigenous communities also plays an important role in the achievement of food security for these communities and others.

27. Establishing sustainable and diverse patterns of production should take into account the present and future needs of the people as well as the natural resources potential and limitations. Policies that provide an effective incentive structure for sustainable management of natural resources will help ensure that national agriculture, fisheries, forestry and natural resources plan and practices are developed and implemented in a holistic approach.

28. Small Island Developing States face the threat of land loss and erosion due to climate changes and sea level rises and have particular needs for their overall sustainable development, improvements in trade, transportation, communication, human resources, stabilization of income and higher export earnings will increase food security in these countries.

29. Food production and rural development, particularly in those countries with significant food security inadequacies, require appropriate and up-to-date technologies which, according to sustainable development criteria and local food traditions, promote modernization of local production methods and facilitate transfer of technology. Full benefit from these technologies will require training, education and skill development programmes for local human resources. National efforts to increase local capacity, coupled with consolidated international cooperation, facilitate application of know-how and technology in areas with similar conditions and new techniques. This may be promoted by active international cooperation, particularly towards developing countries, both at the North-South and South-South levels.

30. Research in agriculture, fisheries and forestry will be essential to achieving the sustainable food productivity increases upon which the short and long term food security of a growing world population will depend. The combination of such research, and an enabling

environment, can improve food security both at national and household levels. Equity issues and equality between women and men should be given appropriate consideration when setting research agendas for the future. Research efforts should clearly focus on poverty eradication and.on the creation of more environmentally sustainable agricultural, fisheries, forestry and food-production systems. This research should be directed to low, as well as high, potential areas according to their specific research needs. Renewed efforts should be made to involve farmers, fishers, foresters and their organizations in setting research priorities and directions, and to make experimental findings accessible to them.

31. The economic and social development of the rural sector is a key requisite for the achievement of food security for all. Rural poverty is a complex phenomenon that varies considerably between and within countries. The rural areas in developing countries are generally poorly equipped in terms of technical and financial resources and educational infrastructure. In these areas, lack of income opportunities, failure to crop and to maintain production systems, inadequate commodity and input and consumer goods distribution networks, limited access to public services and the poor quality of these services are all fundamental aspects that need to be considered with regard to rural food security. The main consequences of this are reflected in high population growth and out-migration, both internally and to other countries.

Objectives and Actions

32. **Objective 3.1** : To pursue, through participatory means, sustainable, intensified and diversified food production, increasing productivity, efficiency, safety gains, pest control and reduced wastes and losses, taking fully into account the need to sustain natural resources.

To this end, governments, in partnership with all actors

of civil society, and with the support of international institutions, will, as appropriate :

(a) Establish policies and implement programmes to optimize, in an economically, socially and environmentally sound manner, sustainable agriculture, fisheries and forestry production, particularly of the main staple foods, aimed at achieving food security;

(b) Promote policies and programmes which encourage appropriate input technologies, farming techniques, and other sustainable methods, such as organic farming, to assist farming operations to become profitable, with the goal of reducing environmental degradation, while creating financial resources within the farming operation; such programmes should, when relevant, build upon farmers' own experiences and indigenous knowledge;

(c) Promote the conservation and sustainable use of biological diversity and its components in terrestrial and marine ecosystem, with a view to enhancing food security, notably through supporting the UN. Convention on Biological Diversity, 1992.

(d) Promote sustainable development in mixed-farming systems and the processing and marketing of diverse food products and by-products, in response to the needs of the consumers for properly balanced diets;

(e) Promote crop and livestock productivity through widespread use of improved seeds and breeds and integrated plant nutrition-system methods, where necessary and ecologically and economically feasible; in addition, seek to achieve lasting fertility improvements in tropical soils;

(f) Promote more efficient and sustainable livestock production systems through the improvement of grazing lands, fodder crops and the use of multiple sources of animal feed;

(g) Promote development of environmentally sound and

sustainable aquaculture well integrated into rural, agricultural and coastal development;

(h) Promote sustainable production and use of food, fodder, fuel and other products derived from forests to enhance food security; such action will also result in increased rural income and employment, thus contributing to sustainable forest management by increasing the value of forests;

(i) Seek to ensure effective prevention and progressive control of plant and animal pests and diseases, including especially those which are of transboundary nature, such as rinderpest, cattle tick, foot and mouth disease and desert locust, where outbreaks can cause major food shortages, destabilize markets and trigger trade measures; and promote concurretly, regional collaboration in plant pests and animal disease control and the widespread development and use of integrated pest management practices.

33. **Objective 3.2** : To combat environmental threats to food security, in particular, drought and desertification, pests, erosion of biological diversity, and degradation of land and aquatic-based natural resources, restore and rehabilitate the natural resource base, including water and watersheds, in depleted and overexploited areas to achieve greater production.

To this end, governments, in partnership with all actor of civil society, and with the support of international institutions, will, as appropriate :

(a) Monitor and promote rehabilitation and conservation of natural resources in food producing areas as well as in adjacent forest lands, non-arable lands, and watersheds; and where necessary upgrade sustainably the productive capacity of these resources; and establish policies that create economic and social incentives to reduce degradation;

(b) Identify the potential and improve the productive use of national land and water resources for sustainable increases in food production, taking into account the anticipated impacts of natural climate variability and climatic change on rainfall and temperature patterns;

(c) Develop appropriate national and regional policies and plans for water and watersheds, and water management techniques; promote, economically, socially and environmentally sound irrigation improvement, in particular small-scale irrigation, and sustainable intensification of rainfed agriculture, with a view to increasing cropping intensities and reducing the impact of droughts and floods on food output and restoring natural resources, while at the same time preserving the quality and availability of water for other purposes, especially human consumption.

(d) Promote early ratification and implementation of the Agreement for Implementation of Instruments of United Nations Convention of the Law of the Sea of 10 December 1982 Relating to the Conservation of Management of Straddling Fish Stocks and Highly Migratory Fish Stocks (the UN Agreement of Straddling Fish Stock and Highly Migratory Fish Stocks) and of the FAO Agreement to Promote Compliance with International Conservation and Management Measures by Fishing Vessels on the High Seas. Implement sustainable fisheries management and practices, in particular the code of Conduct for Responsible Fisheries, to address a responsible and sustainable utilization and conservation of fisheries resources in order to optimize the long-term sustainable contribution of fisheries resources to food security - and fully recognizing Agenda 21, and the Kyoto Declaration and Plan of Action within the context of the relevant rule of International Law as reflected in the United Nations Convention on the Law of the Sea (UNCLOS)[2]-by, *inter alia,* strengthening

[2] Reference in this Plan of Action to UNCLOS, UN Agreement on Stradding Fish Stocks and highly Migratory Fish Stocks, and other International Agreement, do not prejudice the position of any State with respect to signature, ratification or accession to that Convention or to such other agreements.

and establishing, as needed, appropriate regional and sub-regional fisheries management organizations or arrangements, minimizing wastes in fisheries, reducing excess fishing capacity and applying the precautionary approach in accordance with the UN Agreement[3] on Straddling Fish Stocks and Highly Migratory Fish Stocks and the Code of Conduct for Responsible Fisheries; by establishing and strengthening integrated marine and coastal area management; by conserving and sustainably utilizing marine and freshwater biodiversity; and by studying the effectiveness of multispecies management in the context of relevant provisions of UNCLOS and Agenda 21. In working to achieve the above, full recognition should be given to the special circumstances and requirements of developing countries, particularly the least developed among them and the Small Island Developing States;

(e) Promote an integrated approach to conservation and sustainable utilization of plant genetic resources for food and agriculture, through *inter alia* appropriate in *situ* and *ex situ* approaches, systematic surveying and inventorying, approaches to plant breeding which broaden the genetic base of crops, and fair and equitable sharing of benefits arising from the use of such resources;

(f) Promote the conservation and sustainable utilization of animal genetic resources;

(g) Reduce the deforestation rate and increase forest coverage, maintain and develop the multiple contributions of forests, trees and forestry to food security for the conservation and sustainable use of land and water resources, including the protection of watersheds, and as reservoirs of biological diversity; to this end, implement the UNCED outcomes related to forests;

(h) Seek to understand better the impacts of global environmental threats, in particular climate change and

[3] Ibid.

variability, the depletion of the ozone layer, loss of biodiversity and various forms of environmental pollution, on food security;

(i) Implement the Leipzig Global Plan of Action;

(j) Promote early ratification and implementation of United Nations Convention to Combat Desertification in Countries Experiencing Serious Drought and/or Desertification, Particularly in Africa, 1994, and implement the Convention on Biological Diversity, 1992, the Montreal Protocol on Substances that Deplete the Ozone Layer, 1987, and the United Nations Framework Convention on Climate Change, 1992;

(k) Seek to prevent and control degradation and over exploitation of natural resources in poorly endowed, ecologically stressed areas. In those areas critical to the achievement of food security for developing countries, promote and provide location-specific institutional, infrastructural and technical support.

34. **Objective 3.3** : To promote sound policies and programmes on transfer and use of technologies, skills development and training appropriate to the food security needs of developing countries and compatible with sustainable development, particularly in rural and disadvantaged areas.

To this end, governments, in partnership with all actors of civil society, and with the support of international institutions, will, as appropriate :

(a) Strengthen agricultural, fisheries and forestry education, training, skills development and extension systems, ensuring equal gender opportunities and close interaction with research systems and farmers, fishers and foresters, in particular small-scale farmers, fishers and foresters and other food producers, and their representative organizations in food production technology and transfer, and initiate programmes to increase the proportion of women in these systems. National capacity-building efforts, principally in LIFDCs should be supported with North-South and South-South cooperation among education and extension and research institutions;

(b) Promote viable technology transfer and extension services that meet real local needs; stimulate programmes that will help identify possibilities of bilateral and regional cooperation so that experience and technology information can be exchanged on a South-South and North-South level;

(c) Promote means to reduce women farmers' workload by supporting and facilitating access to appropriate productive and domestic labour saving technologies;

(d) Establish policies and programmes for the development and use of technologies that offer economic and ecological benefits and protect the consumer and the environment.

35. **Objective 3.4** : To take decisive action in cooperation between the public and the private sectors to strengthen and broaden research and scientific cooperation in agriculture, fisheries and forestry in supporting policy and international, regional, national and local action to increase productive potential and maintain the natural resource base in agriculture, fisheries and forestry and in support of efforts to eradicate poverty and promote food security.

To this end, governments in collaboration with the international and scientific communities, in both the public and the private sectors, as appropriate, will :

(a) Strengthen national research systems in order to develop coordinated programmes in support of research to promote food security. Such programmes should focus on interdisciplinary research to provide a scientific basis for policies and action to maintain the natural resource base while increasing the productivity potential of agriculture, fisheries, including aquaculture, and forestry. Appropriate attention will be given to areas that are less endowed with natural resources. Increased cooperation with the private sector will be promoted;

(b) Strengthen international research systems, in particular the Consultative Group on International Agricultural Research (CGIAR), and promote coordination and collaboration among international, developed country, and developing country institutions;

(c) Participate actively in and support international cooperation in research to promote food security, in particularly in developing countries, with special emphasis on underutilized food crops in these countries;

(d) Enhance the institutional framework allowing for the full participation of all interested parties, including indigenous people and their communities, local people, consumers, farmers, fishers and foresters and their organizations and the private sector in the identification of research needs;

(e) Promote suitable systems, *inter alia* participatory systems, for the dissemination and extension of research results;

(f) Ensure that gender perspectives are integrated in research planning and implementation;

(g) Promote development of methods and criteria for the strengthening of integrated and policy relevant scientific knowledge;

(h) Promote research and development leading to use, at regional national and local levels, of appropriate technologies, relevant post-harvest and transformation techniques, and adapted plant and animal breeding that meet local needs;

(i) Promote the research needed to continue international efforts to develop, disseminate and apply climate forecast information that will increase sustainable agricultural, fisheries and forestry productivity and be of particular benefit to developing countries.

36. **Objective 3.5** : To formulate and implement integrated rural development strategies, in low and high potential areas, that promote rural employment, skill formation, infrastructure, institutions and services, in support of rural development and household food security and that reinforce the local productive capacity of farmers, fishers and foresters and other actively involved in the food sector, including members of vulnerable and disadvantaged groups, women and indigenous people, and their representative organizations, and that ensure their effective participation.

To this end, governments, in partnership with all actors of civil society, and with the support of international institutions, will as appropriate :

(a) Include in their national social and economic development policies, plans and programmes, actions that will foster the social and economic revitalization of the rural sector, with particular regard to the promotion of investment and employment that will make good use of the rural workforce and to the promotion of political, economic and administrative decentralization;

(b) Strengthen local government institutions in rural areas and provide them with adequate resources, decision-making authority and mechanisms for grassroots participation;

(c) Encourage and enable farmers, fishers and foresters and

other food producers and providers as well as their organizations, particularly small farmers and artisanal fisherfolk, by strengthening institutional structures to define their responsibilities and protect their rights and those of the consumer;

(d) Promote the development and diversification of rural markets, reduce post-harvest losses and ensure safe storage, food processing and distribution facilities and transportation systems;

(e) Reinforce the follow-up to the World Conference on Agrarian Reform and Rural Development (WCARRD), 1979;

(f) Develop and encourage training programmes in sustainable natural resources management.

Governments, in cooperation with the private sector and non-governmental organizations, will :

(g) Develop the technical and educational infrastructure in rural areas;

(h) Promote the development of rural banking, credit and savings schemes, where appropriate, including equal access to credit for men and women, micro-credit for the poor, as well as adequate insurance mechanisms;

(i) Promote food production, processing and marketing systems which increase opportunities for stable, gainful and equal and equitable employment conditions in the food and rural sectors; where appropriate, promote off-farm activities in rural areas combining agriculture, fisheries and forestry production with processing and marketing activities, cottage industries and tourism, particularly in marginal areas and peri-urban areas;

(j) Foster the social and economic organization of the rural population with particular emphasis on the development of small-scale farmers', fishers', and foresters' cooperatives, community organizations and development associations, so that rural inhabitants may be actively involved in decision-making, monitoring and evaluation of rural development programmes;

(k) Recognize farmers', fishers', foresters', rural workers', and consumers' organizations at local, national, regional and international levels and promote a regular dialogue and partnership with their respective governments and their linkage with all appropriate institutions and sectors on sustainable agriculture, fisheries and forestry and sustainable management of natural resources;

(l) Promote the empowerment of small-scale family farmers, fishers and foresters, both women and men, to set up their own cooperatives and business undertakings, as well as farmers' and fishers' financial and mutual institutions;

(m) Enhance cooperation and exchange among farmers, fishers, foresters and their representative organizations, both within and between developing countries, industrialized countries and economies in transition.

Governments, in collaboration with the international community, will :

(n) Develop international South-South technical cooperation programmes that will facilitate the implementation of nutritional programmes that have proved successful in other developing countries;

(o) Implement the outcomes of UNCED, particularly as regards Chapter 14 of Agenda 21.

COMMITMENT FOUR

We will strive to ensure that food, agricultural trade and overall trade policies are conducive to fostering food security for all through a fair and market-oriented world trade system.

The Basis for Action

37. Trade is key element in achieving world food security. Trade generates effective utilization of resources and

stimulates economic growth which is critical to improving food security. Trade allows food consumption to exceed food production, helps to reduce production and consumption fluctuations and relieves part of the burden of stock holding. It has a major bearing on access to food through its positive effect on economic growth, income and employment. Appropriate domestic economic and social policies will better ensure that all, including the poor, will benefit from economic growth. Appropriate trade policies promote the objectives of sustainable growth and food security. It is essential that all members of the World Trade Organization (WTO) respect and fulfil the totality of the undertakings of the Uruguay Round. For this purpose it will be necessary to refrain from unilateral measures not in accordance with WTO obligations.

38. The Uruguay Round Agreement established a new international trade framework that offers opportunity to developed and developing countries to benefit from appropriate trade policies and self-reliance strategies. The progressive implementation of the Uruguay Round as a whole will generate increasing opportunities for trade expansion and economic growth to the benefits of all participants. Therefore, adaptation to the provisions of the various agreements during the implementation period must be ensured. Some least developed and net food-importing developing countries may experience short term negative effects in terms of the availability of adequate supplies of basic foodstuffs from external sources on reasonable terms and conditions, including short term difficulties in financing normal levels of commercial imports of basic foodstuffs. The Decision on Measures Concerning the Possible Negative Effects of the Reform Programme on Least-Developed and Net Food-Importing Developing Countries, Marrakesh 1994, shall be fully implemented.

Objectives and Actions

39. **Objective 4.1** : To meet challenges of and utilize the

opportunities arising from the international trade framework established in recent global and regional trade negotiations.

To this end, governments, in partnership with all actors of civil society, will, as appropriate :

(a) Endeavour to establish, especially in developing countries, well functioning internal marketing and transportation systems to facilitate better links within and between domestic, regional and world markets, and diversity trade;

(b) Seek to ensure that national policies related to international and regional trade agreements do not have an adverse impact on women's new traditional economic activities towards food security.

Members of the WTO will :

(c) Pursue the implementation of the Uruguay Round Agreement which will improve market opportunities for efficient food, agricultural, fisheries and forestry producers and processors, particularly those of developing countries.

The international community, in cooperation with governments and civil society, will, as appropriate :

(d) Continue to assist countries to adjust their institutions and standards both for internal and external trade to food safety and sanitary requirements;

(e) Give full consideration to promote financial and technical assistance to improve the agricultural productivity and infrastructure of developing countries, especially the LIFDCs, in order to optimize the opportunities arising from the international trade framework;

(f) Promote technical assistance and encourage technology transfer consistent with international trade rules, in particular to those developing countries needing it, to meet international standards, so that they are in a position to take advantage of the new market opportunities;

(g) Endeavour to ensure mutual supportiveness of trade and environment policies in support of sustainable food security, looking to the WTO to address the relationship between WTO provisions and trade measures for environment purposes, in conformity with the provisions of the Ministerial Decision on Trade and Environment in the Uruguay Round Agreement, and make every effort to ensure that environmental measures, do not unfairly affect market access for developing countries' food and agricultural exports;

(h) Conduct international trade in fish and fishery products in a sustainable manner in accordance, as appropriate, with the principles, rights and obligations established in World Trade Organization (WTO) Agreement, the UN Agreement on Straddling Fish Stocks and Highly Migratory Fish Stocks, the Code of Conduct for Responsible Fisheries and other relevant international agreements.

40. **Objective 4.2** : To meet essential food import needs in all countries, considering world price and supply fluctuations and taking especially into account food consumption levels of vulnerable groups in developing countries.

To this end, governments and the international community will, as appropriate :

(a) Recognizing the effects of world price fluctuations, examine WTO, compatible options and take any appropriate steps to safeguard the ability of importing developing countries, especially LIFDCs, to purchase adequate supplies of basic food stuffs from external sources on reasonable terms and conditions.

Food exporting countries should :

(b) Act as reliable sources of supplies to their trading partners and give due consideration to the food security of importing countries especially the LIFDCs;

(c) Reduce subsidies on food exports in conformity with the Urguay Round Agreement in the context of the ongoing process of reform in agriculture conducted in the WTO;

(d) Administer all export related trade policies and programmes reasonably, with a view to avoiding disruptions in world food and agriculture import and export markets, in order to improve the environment to enhance supplies, production and food security, especially in developing countries;

Members of the WTO will :

(e) Fully implement the Decision on Measures Concerning the Possible Negative Effects of the Reform Programme on Least-Developed and Net Food-Importing Developing Countries through the WTO Committee on Agriculture and encourage international financial institutions, where appropriate, to help least-developed and net food-improting developing countries to meet short-term difficulties in financing essential food imports;

(f) Refrain from using export restrictions in accordance with Article 12 of the WTO Agreement on Agriculture;

International organizations and particularly FAO, will :

(g) Continue to monitor closely and inform member nations of developments in world food prices and stocks.

41. **Objective 4.3** : To support the continuation of the reform process in conformity with the Uruguay Round Agreement, particularly Article 20 of the Agreement on Agriculture.

In this end, government will, as appropriate :

(a) Promote the national and regional food security policies and programmes of developing countries particularly in regard to their staple food supplies;

(b) Support the continuation of the reform process in conformity with the Uruguay Round Agreement and ensure that developing countries are well informed and equal partners in the process, working for effective solutions that improve their access to markets and are conducive to the achievement of sustainable food security.

International organizations, including FAO, will, according to their respective mandates :

(c) Continue to assist developing countries in preparing for multilateral trade negotiations including in agriculture, fisheries and forestry *inter alia* through studies, analysis and training.

COMMITMENT FIVE

We will endeavour to prevent and be prepared for natural disasters and man-made emergencies and to meet transitory and emergency food requirements in ways that encourage recovery, rehabilitation, development and a capacity to satisfy future needs.

The Basis for Action

42. While the number of people affected by natural disastes fluctuates annually, there has been a dramatic increase in the number of victims of civil conflicts. These situations require emergency assistance and they point to the importance of early action to diffuse tensions and of preparedness in minimizing the risk of future crises and in preventing food emergencies.

43. National and international relief operations are often the only solution for hungry people facing immediate starvation, and should continue to be a priority and be provided in an impartial and political manner, with due respect to national sovereignty and in accordance with the charter of the United Nations and the guiding principles of the UN General Assembly (UNGA) Resolution 46/182. However, emergency food assistance cannot be a basis for sustainable food security. Conflict prevention

and resolution, and stepped up rehabilitation and development promotion activities, which prevent recurrence of and reduce vulnerability to food emergencies, are essential elements of food security. Emergency preparedness is a central element for minimizing the negative effects of food emergencies and famines.

Objectives and Actions

44. **Objective 5.1**: To reduce demands for emergency food assistance through enhancing efforts to prevent and resolve man-made emergencies, particularly international, national and local conflicts.

To this end, governments individually and collectively, and in partnership with all actors of civil society, will:

(a) Use appropriate international, regional and national mechanisms to prevent or reduce those situations, in particular war and civil conflict, which gave rise to man-made emergencies and increase demands for emergency assistance, including food aid;

(b) Coordinate policies, action and legal instrument and/or measures to combat terrorism and other activities contrary to human rights and human dignity;

(c) Promote the continuation of international discussions and cooperation on all aspects of anti-personnel land mines.

45. Objective 5.2 : To establish as quickly as possible prevention and preparedness strategies for LIFDCs and other countries and regions vulnerable to emergencies.

To this end, governments, in partnership with all actors of civil society and with international organizations where necessary, will, as appropriate:

(a) Prepare and/or maintain for each LIFDC, and other countries and regions vulnerable to emergencies, vulnerability information and mapping, drawing on, amongest others, a food insecurity and vulnerability information and mapping system, once established, with an analysis of the major causes of vulnerability and their consequences, making maximum use of existing data and information systems to avoid duplication to effort;

(b) Maintain, promote and establish, as quickly as possible, in collaboration with non-governmental organizations and other organizations, as appropriate, the preparedness strategies and mechanisms agreed upon at the ICN, including the development and application of climate forecast information for surveillance and early-warming, drought, flood, other natural disasters, pest and disease alertness;

(c) Support international efforts to develop and apply climate forecast information to improve the effectiveness and efficiency of emergency preparedness and response activities, with special efforts to create synergy and avoid duplication;

(d) Promote the development of appropriate community-based and regional surveillance systems to gather and asses information and to implement prevention and preparedness programmes.

46. **Objective 5.3** : To improve and, if neccessary, develop efficient and effective emergency response mechanisms at international, regional, national and local levels.

To this end, international organizations, in close cooperation with governments and civil society, as appropriate, will:

(a) Strengthen the coordination and efficiency of international emergency assistance to ensure rapid, coordinated and appropriate response, particularly by improving communication amongest the international community.

Governments, in partnership with all actors of civil society, will, as appropriate:

(b) Seek to ensure adequate supervision of emergency operations and involve communities, local authorities and institutions and grassroots relief initiatives and structures in implementing emergency operations to better identify and reach populations and areas at greatest risk. Women should be fully involved in the assessment of needs and in the management and evaluation or relief operations;

(c) Pursue at local and national levels, as appropriate, adequate and cost-effective strategic emergency food security reserve policies programmes;

(d) Promote triangular food aid operations;

(e) Project the lives of civil populations, including humanitarian aid workers, in times of conflict;

(f) Seek to ensure that access to food, with particular attention to women headed households, is protected during emergency situations;

(g) Consider the creation of national volunteers corps, building upon "White Helmets", as defined by UNGA Resolutions 49/139B and 50/19, and already launched by the United Nations Volunteers(UNV), in order to support emergency relief and rehabilitation operations when deemed pertinent and in accordance with the guiding principles on humanitarian assistance embodied in UNGA Resolution 46/182.

47. Objective 5.4 : To strengthen linkages between relief operations and development programmes, along with demining activities where necessary, so that they are mutually supportive and facilitate the transition from relief to development.

To this end , international organizations, governments and civil society will, as appropriate:

(a) Keep under review the standards for the nutritional adequacy of food assistance to disaster-affected populations;

(b) Ensure that emergency operations will foster the transition from relief, through recovery, to development;

(c) Prepare and pursue well-planned post-emergency rehabilitation and development programmes to re-establish the capacity of households, including those headed by women, to meet their basic needs in the long term, as well as to rebuild national production capacity and return to sustainable economic development and social progress as soon as possible. Where necessary, these should include operations to remove land mines.

COMMITMENT SIX

We will promote allocation and use of public and private investments to foster human resources, sustainable food, agriculture, fisheries and forestry systems, and rural development, in high and low potential areas.

The Basis for Action

48. Many developing countries need to reverse the recent neglect of investment in agriculture and rural development and mobilize sufficient investment resources to support sustainable food security and diversified rural development. A sound policy environment, in which such food-related investment can fulfil its potential, is essential. Most of the resources required for investment will be generated from domestic, private and public resources. Governments should provide an economic and legal framework which promotes efficient markets that encourage private sector mobilization of savings, investment and capital formation. They should also devote and appropriate proportion of their expenditure to

investments which enhance sustainable food security.

49. The international community has a key role to play in supporting the adoption of appropriate national polices and, where necessary and appropriate, in providing technical and financial assistance to assist developing countries and countries with economies in transition in fostering food security. Foreign Direct Investment (FDI) and other private financial flows have increased considerably recently and provide an important source of external resources. Official Development Assistance (ODA) has exhibited a decline in recent years. In the context of food security, ODA is of critical importance, particularly for countries and sectors left aside by other external sources of finance.

50. All partners in development, including investors and donors, should place priority on sectors of developing countries' economies relating to food security. To this end, governments should adopt policies that promote foreign and domestic direct investment and effective use of development assistance.

51. In view of their special situation, Small Island Developing States have identified key sectors of priority which require investment so as to achieve their sustainable development.

Objectives and Actions

52. **Objective 6.1** : To create the policy framework and conditions so that optimal public and private investments are encouraged in equitable and sustainable development of the food systems, rural development and human resources on the scale needed to contribute to food security.

To this end, governments, in cooperation with all actors of civil society international and private financing institutions and technical assistance agencies will, appropriate:

(a) Promote policies and measures to enhance the flow and effectiveness of investment for food security;

(b) Give priority to human resource development and strengthen public institutions, especially in LIFDCs, including through equipping and staff training, to enhance their supportive and facilitating role in promoting increased investment in food security;

(c) Encourage the development of public-private partnership and other institutions in promoting socially and environmentally responsible investment and re-investment from domestic and foreign resources, and increase the participation of local communities in investment;

(d) Strengthen cooperation, at the regional and international level, to share the costs of investments in areas of common interest, such as appropriate technology generation through collaborative research and transfer, as well as to share investment experience and best practices.

53. **Objective 6.2** : To endeavor to mobilize, and optimize the use of technical and financial resources from all sources, including debt relief, in order to raise investment in activities related to sustainable agriculture, fisheries, forestry and food production in developing countries to the levels needed to contribute to food security.

To this end, governments, in cooperation with the international community and all actors of civil society, as well as international and private financing institutions will, as appropriate:

(a) Undertake to raise sufficient and stable funding from private and public domestic and foreign sources to achieve and sustain food security;

(b) Encourage investment to create infrastructures and management systems that facilitate sustainable utilization and management of water resources;

(c) Support investment that contribute to sustainable food security and further conservation and sustainable utilization and management of natural resources, including land, water, watersheds, fisheries and forests;

(d) Strive to secure appropriate international financial assistance for sectors related to food security, where it is needed;

(e) Strengthen efforts towards the fulfilment of the agreed ODA target of 0.7% of GNP. In striving to promote sustainable food security, development partners should endeavour to mobilize, and optimize the use of technical and financial resources at the levels needed to contribute to this goal and should ensure that this flow of concessional funding is directed to economically and environmentally sustainable activities;

(f) Focus ODA towards countries that have a real need for it, especially low-income countries, and enhance their capacity to utilize it effectively;

(g) Explore new ways of mobilizing public and private financial resources for food security, *inter alia*, through the appropriate reduction of excessive military expenditures, including global military expenditures and the arms trade, and investment for arms production and acquisition, taking into consideration national security requirements;

(h) Promote mechanisms to mobilize domestic savings, including rural savings;

(i) Promote mechanisms to provide access to adequate credit, including micro-credit, for men and women equally, for activities in the food sector;

(j) Promote investment to benefit small-scale food producers, especially women, and their organizations, in food security programmes; Strengthen their capacity to design and implement these programmes;

(k) Give priority to people-centered investments in education, health and nutrition in order to promote broad based economic growth and sustainable food security;

(l) Identify financial, physical and technical resources available internationally and encourage the enhancement of their transfer, where appropriate, into developing countries and countries with economies in transition while also developing and enabling environment, notably through strengthening national capacities including human resources;

(m) Intensify the search for practical and effective solutions to debt problems of developing countries and support the recent initiatives of international financial institutions (International Monetary Fund and World Bank), to reduce the total external burden of Heavily Indebted Poor Countries;

(n) Explore the possibilities for countries to direct the funds released debt swaps towards the achievement of food security.

COMMITMENT SEVEN

We will implement, monitor, and follow-up this Plan of Action at all levels in cooperation with the international community.

The Basis for Action

54. World food security is of concern to all members of the international community because of its increasing interdependence with respect to issues such as political stability and peace, poverty eradication, prevention of and reaction to crises and disasters, environmental degradation, trade, global threats to the sustainability of food security, growing world population, trans-border population movements, and technology, research, investment, and financial cooperation.

55. National, regional and international mechanisms for political, financial and technical cooperation should be focused on the earliest possible achievement of sustainable world food security.

56. Governments have the primary responsibility for creating an economic and political environment that assures the food security of their citizens, involving for this purpose all elements of civil society. The international community, and the UN system, including FAO, as well as other agencies and bodies according to their mandates, have important contributions to offer to the goal of food security for all.

57. The multi-dimensional nature of the follow-up to the World food Summit includes actions at the national, intergovernmental and inter-agency levels. In addition to the indispensible mobilization of national efforts, the effective implementation of the World food Summit Plan of Action requires strong international cooperation and a monitoring process at the national, regional and global levels, using existing mechanisms and fora for its operation. To allow for better cooperation, the information regarding the different actors in the field of food security and agriculture, fisheries, forestry and rural development and their activities and resources needs to be improved, where appropriate. Setting realistic targets and monitoring progress towards them call for reliable and relevant information and analysis which are still often unavailaible at the national and international levels. For the follow-up to the World Food Summit, coordination and cooperation within UN system, including the Bretton Woods institutions, is vital and should take into account the mandate of FAO and other relevant organizations. Bearing in mind UNGA Resolution 50/109, the outcome of the World Food Summit should be included in the follow-up to major international UN conferences and summits, including the implementation of their respective programmes of action in conformity with UNGA Resolution 50/227 and ESCOSOC Resolution 1996/36, in order to

promote sustainable food security for all as a fundamental element of the UN systems's effort to eradicate poverty. In this context, the implementation of the World Food Summit Plan of Action requires actions at the inter-governmental level, in particular through the CFS and at the inter-agency level through the Administrative Committee on Coordination (ACC). In the field, the representatives of all UN agencies should work within the UN resident coordinators' system to support country-level implementation of the World Food Summit Plan of Action.

Objectives and Actions

58. **Objective 7.1** : To adopt actions within each country's national framework to enhance food security and enable the implementation of the Commitments of the World Food Summit Plan of Action.

To this end, governments will, where appropriate:

(a) Review and revise, as appropriate, their national plans, programmes and strategies with a view to achieving food security consistent with the World Food Summit commitments;

(b) Establish or improve national mechanisms to set priorities, develop, implement and monitor the components of action for food security within designated time frames, based both on national and local needs, and provide the necessary resources for their functioning;

(c) In collaboration with civil society, formulate the launch national Food for All Campaigns to mobilize all stakeholders at all levels of society and their resources in each country, in support of the implementation of the World Food Summit Plan of Action;

(d) Actively encourage a greater role for, and alliances with, civil society organizations in addressing food security;

(e) Strive to mobilize public and private resources to support community food security initiatives;

(f) Establish mechanisms to collect information on the nutritional status of all members of communities, especially the poor, women, children and members of vulnerable and disadvantaged groups, to monitor and improve their household food security;

(g) Complement existing national plans of action on nutrition, developed as a follow-up to the ICN, with action on relevant aspects of food security or, where necessary, develop such plans in accordance with the recommendations of this Summit and the ICN, in partnership with all actors of civil society;

(h) Plan and monitor in a coordinated manner the implementation of relevant recommendations of all UN conferences aimed at eradicating poverty and improving food security and nutrition.

59. **Objective 7.2** : To improve sub-regional, regional, and international cooperation and to mobilize, and optimize the use of available resources to support national efforts for the earliest possible achievement of sustainable world food security.

To this end, governments, in cooperation among themselves and with international institutions, using information on food insecurity and vulnerability, including mapping, will, as appropriate:

(a) Reinforce poverty eradication strategies and orient the development assistance policies of the international agencies of the UN system, with broad participation of the developing countries, so that resources are directed towards sustainable development, including agriculture for food security, and effectively contribute to the improved situation of food insecure households;

(b) Encourage relevant agencies within the UN system to

initiate, *inter alia* within the framework of the ACC, consultations on the further elaboration and definition of a food insecurity and vulnerability information and mapping system to be developed in a coordinated manner; member countries and their institutions and other organizations, as appropriate, should be included in the development, operation and use of the system; FAO should play a catalytic role in this effort, within the framework of the ad hoc inter-agency task forces on the follow-up of the UN conferences. The result of that work should be reported to the UN Economic and Social Council (ECOSOC) through the ACC;

(c) Improve the collection, through definition of common standards, and the analysis, dissemination and utilization of information and data, disaggregated *inter alia* by gender, needed to guide and monitor progress towards the achievement of food security; in this context, the contribution of NGOs is recognized;

(d) Continue, within the framework of UNGA resolutions 50/120, 50/227 and the coordinated follow-up by the UN system to the major UN conferences and summits since 1990, the review of functions and capacities of the UN system, including the specialized agencies, programmes and funds, in their relation to food security; this review should aim at reducing duplications and filling gaps in coverage, defining the tasks of each organization within its mandate, making concrete proposals for their strengthening and for improving coordination with governments, and for avoiding duplication of work between relevant organizations, and implement these proposals as a matter of urgency;

(e) Starting in 1997, review the adequacy and effectiveness of the allocation and use of financial and human resources for action required to ensure food for all as a follow-up to the World Food Summit, and reallocate available resources accordingly, with special reference to the needs of countries facing deteriorating food security, nutrition, health and resource degradation;

(f) Review and streamline existing mechanisms, increase cooperation and the sharing of knowledge and experience among developing countries and with developed countries, and improve coordination amongst and between all partners involved in order to maximize synergy for the attainment of food security;

(g) Focus technical assistance more effectively on building up and mobilizing national capacity, expertise and local institutions;

(h) Invite the ACC through its Chairman, the Secretary General of the UN, to ensure appropriate inter-agency coordination in accordance with UNGA Resolution 50/227 and, when considering the Chair of any ACC mechanisms for inter-agency follow-up to the World Food Summit, to reorganize, in the spirit of ECOSOC, Resolution 1996/36, the major role of FAO in the Field of food security, within its mandate.

With clear tasks given to each within its mandate and under system-wide coordination within the framework of the coordinated follow-up to UN conferences, in accordance with UNGA Resolution 50/120, FAO and the other relevant organizations of the UN system, as well as the international finance and trade institutions and other international and regional technical assistance organizations, are invited to :

(i) On request, assist countries in reviewing and formulating national plans of action including targets, goals and timetables for achieving food security;

(j) Facilitate a coherent and coordinated UN system follow-up to the World Food Summit at the field level, through the resident coordinators, in full consultation with governments, and in coordination with international financial institutions;

(k) Provide technical assistance to member countries to

facilitate implementation of food security programmes in order to meet targets established by governments;

(l) Assist in arranging partnership for economic and technical cooperation among countries on food security;

(m) Raise the global profile of food security issues through UN systemwide advocacy and sustain the World Food Summit commitments to world food security.

In cooperation among themselves, governments and international financial institutions will:

(n) Make every effort to ensure that goals and programmes aimed at food security and poverty eradication are safeguarded in difficult times of economic transition, budget austerity and structural adjustment;

(o) Encourage the multilateral development banks to enhance their support of developing country efforts to increase food security, especially in Africa.

60. **Objective 7.3** : To monitor actively the implementation of the World Food Summit Plan of Action.

To this end, governments, in partnership with all actors of civil society, in coordination with relevant international institutions and, in conformity with ECOSOC Resolution 1996/36 on the follow-up to the major international UN conferences and summits as appropriate, will:

(a) Establish, through the CFS, a timetable, procedures and standardized reporting formats, which do not duplicate similar reports to the UN, FAO and other agencies, on the national, sub-regional and regional implementation of the World Food Summit Plan of Action;

(b) Set out in the CFS a process for developing targets and verified indicators of national and global food security where they do not exist;

(c) Report to the CFS on national, sub-regional and regional implementation of the World Food Summit Plan of Action, drawing on a food insecurity and vulnerability information and mapping system, once established, as an analytical aid;

(d) Invite the Secretary-General of the UN to request the ACC to report to ECOSOC in accordance with established procedures progress on the follow-up by UN agencies to the World Food Summit;

(e) Monitor through the CFS the national, sub-regional and international implementation of the World Food Summit Plan of Action, using reports from national governments, reports on UN agency follow-up and inter-agency coordination, and information from other relevant international institutions;

(f) Provide regular reports on implementation of the World Food Summit Plan of Action through the CFS via the FAO Council to ECOSOC;

(g) Encourage the effective participation of relevant actors of civil society in the CFS monitoring process, recognizing their critical role in enhancing food security;

(h) By 2006, undertake, in the CFS and within available resources, a major broad-based progress assessment of the implementation of the World Food Summit Plan of Action and a mid-term review of achieving the target of reducing the number of undernourished people to half their present level no later than 2015. This progress assessment and review should be in the context of a special forum of a regular session of the CFS and involve active participation from governments, relevant international organizations and actors of civil society.

61. **Objective 7.4** : To clarify the content of the right to adequate food and the fundamental right of everyone to be free from hunger, as stated in the International Covenant on Economic, Social and Cultural Rights and other relevant international

and regional instruments, and to give particular attention to implementation and full and progressive realization of this right as a means of achieving food security for all.

To this end, governments, in partnership with all actors of civil society, will, as appropriate:

(a) Make every effort to implement the provisions of Article 11 of the International Covenant on Economic, Social and Cultural Rights (the Covenant) and relevant provisions of other international and regional instruments;

(b) Urge States that are not yet Parties to the Covenant to adhere to the Covenant at the earliest possible time;

(c) Invite the Committee on Economic, Social and Cultural Rights to give particular attention to this Plan of Action in the framework of its activities and to continue to monitor the implementation of the specific measures provided for in Article 11 of the Covenant;

(d) Invite relevant treaty bodies and appropriate specialized agencies of the UN to consider how they might contribute, within the framework of the coordinated follow-up by the UN system to the major international UN conferences and summits, including the World Conference on Human Rights, Vienna 1993, within the scope of their mandates, to the further implementation of this right;

(e) Invite the UN High Commissioner for Human rights, in consultation with relevant treaty bodies, and in collaboration with relevant specialized agencies and programmes of the UN system and appropriate intergovernmental mechanisms, to better define the rights related to food in Article 11 of the Covenant and to propose ways to implement and realize these rights as a means of achieving the commitments and objectives of the World Food Summit, taking into account the possibility of formulating voluntary guidelines for food security for all.

62. **Objective 7.5** : To share responsibilities in achieving food security for all so that implementations of the World Food Summit Plan of Action takes place at the lowest possible level at which its purpose could be best achieved.

In implementing this Plan of Action, it is recognized that :

(a) Individuals and households have a key role in decisions and actions affecting their food security. They must be enabled and encouraged to participate actively, both individually and also collectively, through producers, consumers and other organizations of civil society;

(b) Governments have the responsibility to ensure an enabling environment conducive to the achievement of food security;

(c) Regional cooperation takes advantage of geographic complementaries within regions and of economies of scale;

(d) In view of growing interdependence between nations and regions, international cooperation and solidarity between areas experiencing different levels of development are indispensable to achieving food security for all.

The texts of Rome Declaration on World Food Security and World Food Summit Plan of Action were approved by the Committee on World Food Security and submitted to the World Food Summit for adoption.